P

Managing the Unmanageable

"This innovative guide to motivating the toughest members of your team will inspire managers in every setting. With passion, common sense, and clarity, Anne Loehr and Jezra Kaye demystify what makes employees 'unmanageable,' and show, step-by-step, how to turn them around."

—Tom Ward, managing director, The Leland C. and Mary M. Pillsbury Institute for Hospitality Entrepreneurship, Cornell University School of Hotel Administration

"Finally—a really practical approach to dealing with unproductive employee behavior and how to evaluate the cost/benefit of making the effort to turn it around. I wish I'd had this book in my management tool kit twenty years ago. Loehr and Kaye provide an effective, no-nonsense method for engaging in the work of turning an unmanageable, subversive employee into a productive team member that also results in gaining valuable insights into your own management style."

—Christine Salem, managing director, *Outside's Go* magazine

"Whether you're leading a group, spearheading a project, or wondering what happened to a formerly great colleague, this book is a must-read. But be warned: Once you start *Managing the Unmanageable*, you won't be able to put it down! The powerful and invaluable ideas that pour from each page will help you analyze, understand, and stop disruptive behaviors by successfully engaging even the most unmanageable employee."

—Cynthia de Lorenzi, CEO, Success in the City

"**Managing the Unmanageable** brings into clear focus one of the issues many otherwise successful executives simply ignore—the problem employee. This book provides a compelling call to action to not ignore that person, and then it clearly presents a proven, non-threatening method to help both the manager and the employee become a star. Applying these techniques quickly cleared up a lingering problem for me."

—Scott Thacker, COO, Ivory Consulting Corporation

"Where were Anne Loehr and Jezra Kaye when I needed them?! Before starting Savvy Navigator Tours, I managed hundreds of airline industry employees, and this book could have saved me a lot of headaches! Read it now—it's vital to your own and your team's success!"

—Jeffrey Ward, owner, Savvy Navigator Tours

"Having worked with both Loehr and Kaye to successfully hit my company's targeted goals, hone my management skills, and advance my communication, I knew the value of their work and saw the direct, positive impact of their ideas on my company's bottom line. This book was what I expected from their style: a practical, step-by-step, and often humorous guide to handling difficult employees."

—Steve Goldenberg, CEO, Interfolio

MANAGING THE UNMANAGEABLE

How to Motivate Even the Most Unruly Employee

ANNE LOEHR

AND

JEZRA KAYE

Pompton Plains, NJ

MANAGING THE UNMANAGEABLE
EDITED BY JODI BRANDON
TYPESET BY GINA TALUCCI
Cover design by Wes Youssi
Printed in the U.S.A.

To order this title, please call toll-free 1-800-CAREER-1 (NJ and Canada: 201-848-0310) to order using VISA or MasterCard, or for further information on books from Career Press.

The Career Press, Inc.
220 West Parkway, Unit 12
Pompton Plains, NJ 07444
www.careerpress.com

Library of Congress Cataloging-in-Publication Data

CIP Data Available Upon Request.

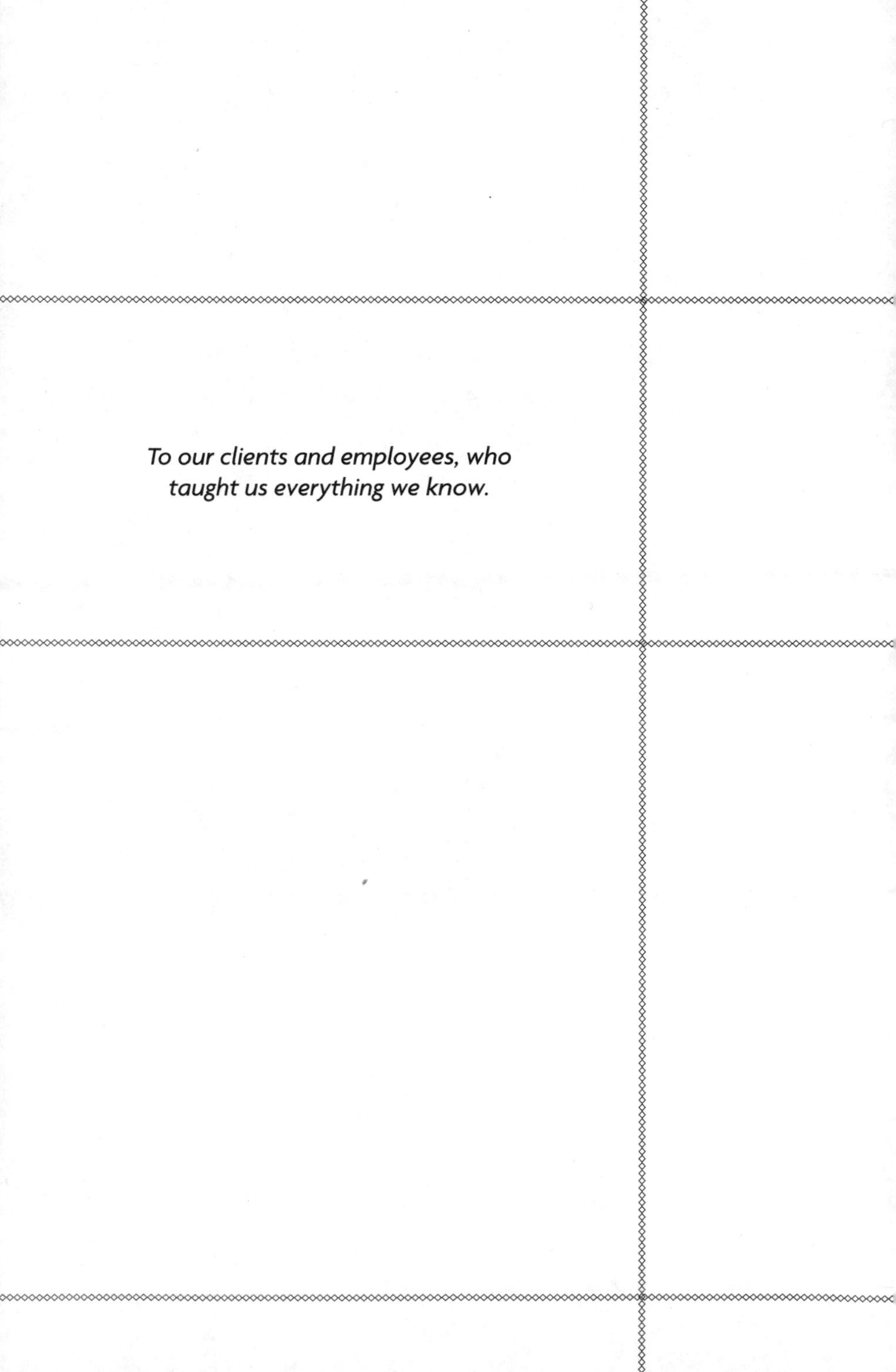

To our clients and employees, who taught us everything we know.

Acknowledgments

We have each been fortunate beyond words to work with dedicated mentors, talented teams, and generous colleagues who have pushed, prodded, and helped shape us into more powerful leaders and better human beings. Naming each of you would be impossible, but we'd like to acknowledge those people without whom this book would not have seen the light of day:

Our partners in learning: Joan Fletcher of Winning Ways, whose input set us on the track, and Rose Rubin Rivera, whose support helped keep us there.

Our agent, Grace Freedson, and our editors, Kirsten Dalley and Jodi Brandon, who guided us through this publishing adventure.

Our parents, siblings, nieces, nephews, and cousins, who love us unstintingly and kick our butts when we need it.

Finally, to our wonderful husbands and daughters—Neel and Ariana Inamdar; Jerome Harris and Laurika Harris-Kaye: You cheered us on (or at least put up with us!) through long days and nights of brainstorming, writing, editing, and hair-tearing. *Thank you* for your love, strength, support, and encouragement. We hope you know that we believe in you every bit as deeply as you believe in us.

Contents

Preface

This book is the result of two very different journeys.

Anne's first management experience was in East Africa. She and her husband had both just graduated from Cornell University's School of Hotel Administration. Eager to test their skills in the world, they seized the chance to run the Turtle Bay Beach Club, a dilapidated 300-bed hotel in the tiny town of Watamu, Kenya. The caveat was they had to sell it in two years, at a profit!

Although Anne's husband had grown up in Kenya, she didn't know one safari animal from another. Yet there she was, a general manager with 12 male, Kenyan direct reports. These department managers were all older than she, and none of them had graduated from high school.

Meanwhile, Jezra was working as a jazz singer in Boston. After 18 years of following that dream, she moved to New York City and decided to pursue a career in corporate marketing communications. While Anne was wrestling with creating a modern hotel management system from scratch, Jezra was writing hundreds of speeches, delivering her own keynote addresses, and coaching executives and employees on how to communicate with audiences and each other. She learned that clear and respectful communications have tremendous power, and when she launched her own thriving communications coaching practice, she learned that these skills can be *taught*.

In 2003, Anne came back from Africa with a fully formed business philosophy and a set of successful coaching and training practices that she has used to coach hundreds of executives, managers, and employees in the military, non-profit, and private sectors. At the core of her success is the knowledge that *attitude* is the best predictor of a group's performance; that treating individuals with respect is the best way to nurture a good attitude; and that, under the right circumstances, *everyone* has a contribution to make.

Of course, the reverse is also true. When circumstances change, or when contributions are blocked, even the best employee can feel frustrated...can act inappropriately...and can, ultimately, become "unmanageable." Turning that situation around is what *Managing the Unmanageable* is all about.

Anne Loehr, Reston, Virginia
Jezra Kaye, Brooklyn, New York

Introduction

This book is about managing an employee's bad behavior.

Not bad behavior in the criminal sense, but behavior that is costly, disruptive, divisive—trouble. If you purchased this book, there's a good chance that you're seeing this kind of behavior in your own organization: Employees who are rude. Egomaniacs. Slackers. Employees who go AWOL when you need them, miss their deadlines, screw up assignments, chase away clients, and fracture your team's morale. The list could probably go on forever, because there seems to be no end to the new and creative ways that employees can find to become unmanageable.

These behaviors—the ones that are worse than petty irritants but don't quite justify dismissal (or jail time)—can be a nightmare for managers. In fact, the very word *unmanageable*, which is used by so many of the executives and managers we both coach, suggests that these behaviors (and the employees who indulge in them) literally can't be managed.

If that's true—if unmanageability is a true dead end—then all of your options are pretty grim. You can fire the employee and start from scratch with someone else. But that can cost a great deal of money, and may not turn out to be an improvement. You can try to tolerate your unmanageable's behavior, which is somewhat like tolerating a snake attack, or an earthquake that measures 9.0 on the Richter scale. Or you can keep banging your head against the wall, trying to change your unmanageable employee (for expediency's sake, we'll call him your "UE" from now on), when neither of you really believes that change is even possible.

Fortunately, there's another option—because it turns out that most "unmanageable" employees aren't really hopeless after all. Yes, some of them truly *are* unmanageable: The vicious or destructive person. The serial sexual harasser. The person who lies, steals, and tries to arrange for someone else to take the fall. These people are true incorrigibles. Even if you could change them, you probably wouldn't want to do it.

But most employees don't fit that mold. What about the UE who used to be good at her job? Or the UE who has a unique skill that you can't afford to throw away? Or the one that your gut tells you still *wants* to be part of your team and somehow make a contribution? These "unmanageables" are like the famous wolf in sheep's clothing, except in reverse. Their skills, positive qualities, and future promise are being temporarily obscured beneath the cloak of unmanageability they're wearing. If you can get them to take off the wolf suit, you just might have a good employee on your hands.

Person in a Wolf Suit? Or Canary in the Coal Mine?

While we're using analogies from the animal kingdom, there is also another possibility to be faced. It's possible that your UE is actually doing you a "favor" by clumsily hinting at deeper, more pervasive issues on your team, in your department, or throughout your entire organization.

"Some favor!," you're probably thinking, and you're right to be suspicious. But what if your UE's challenging and irritating behavior is not the *real* problem in your department or team? What if it results from—and signals—a deeper problem that wouldn't improve even if this particular UE walked out the door?

In the last century, coal miners routinely took caged canaries underground with them, knowing that the canary would react more quickly to diminishing levels of oxygen in a mine than they themselves would. In other words, if the canary keeled over, they knew it was time to get out of there—fast! It's sometimes the case that, like a canary in a coal mine, your UE is acting out because he or she is more sensitive to a negative dynamic on your team than other people are.

This was the case for one of Anne's clients, Eduardo. Eduardo consulted with Anne about how to "fix" an employee named Shibani, a mid-level manager in the non-profit organization that Eduardo ran. When Anne asked what Shibani's challenges were, Eduardo said, "She doesn't communicate well, she misses her deadlines, and she doesn't understand the team vision." Eduardo was convinced that his team's recent lackluster performance was entirely due to Shibani's failings. But as Anne started unraveling the facts, she discovered that there were many issues to be dealt with, not just one. These issues included some realities that Eduardo hadn't recognized yet, such as the fact that his entire team's working practices were substandard, and that people were demoralized from having recently lost a key player. Yes, Shibani's behavior was a problem, but that was largely because she didn't understand her role on the team—and she wasn't the only one. In addition, Eduardo's directions often confused her (again, she wasn't the only one!), so Shibani wasn't able to contribute fully.

If Anne had only worked on Shibani's behavioral challenges, and ignored the context in which they occurred, Eduardo would have missed an opportunity to strengthen other aspects of his team's cohesion and his own performance as a manager. And if that had happened, it's likely that similar problems with communications, priorities, and goals would have surfaced at some later point, when someone else became unmanageable. But by looking at the team holistically, and recognizing that Shibani's role was that of "canary in the coal mine," Anne and Eduardo were able to devise a plan that resolved his team's chronic problems, and strengthened his leadership abilities.

The moral of this story is: Avoid jumping to conclusions or taking things at face value when you're presented with an unmanageable employee. Instead, keep an open mind, ask questions, and think about *what's motivating your UE* before you decide on an action plan.

Please, Fix It Now!

We totally understand that you're busy, or even overwhelmed. You've already spent time, energy, and resources trying to fix your employee, all to no avail. So you probably picked up this book in hopes that we'd tell you how to magically turn your UE "wolf" (or werewolf!) back into a full-fledged (human) member of your team—preferably in the next five minutes. You're looking for a simple process that never fails, complete with instructions for what to do about anything that could possibly go wrong along the way.

Boy, do we wish we could give you that! But there is no such book, because, unfortunately, *there are no cookie-cutter solutions* when it comes to people. Managing people is a complex skill that takes time and endless patience to master. At the heart of that skill is the ability to look at the person in front of you, determine what you're seeing, create a strategy for dealing with him, and then follow through—flexibly, but with relentless persistence.

That's what this book will teach you to do. In its pages, you're going to meet many unmanageable characters. Many of these UEs are composites, but some are real people who jumped straight out of our combined 35 years of management and coaching experience. You'll find out how we, or the managers we coach and advise, turned these failing employees around and helped them achieve manageability and success. You'll learn principles, strategies, and techniques for kicking unmanageable butt (and we mean that in the nicest possible way). But you won't learn quick fixes because, unfortunately, there aren't any.

No Two Are Alike

As you meet each of the employees in this book, and compare them with your own UEs, you're going to notice that they don't always match up. This won't come as a big surprise, because if two 6-year-olds aren't the same, and two CEOs aren't the same, and two athletes aren't the same, why would two UEs be the same, even if they're both Slackers, or Wallflowers, or Grumblers?

In fact, we could have fleshed out a thousand different unmanageable characters in this book and still not have described the one that you want to strangle right now. So don't be concerned if you find yourself thinking, *"I've got a Loose Cannon, but she doesn't act like* this *guy"* or "My *UE isn't described in the book. Does that mean there's no solution for him?"* It doesn't mean anything of the kind, because there's always a solution to unmanageability—one way or the other!

Although you're ultimately the one who'll have to figure out what that solution is, the good news is, we're going to show you how. We're going to arm you with the framework, strategies, tools, and insights you need to handle any UE, and to confidently transform any unmanageable situation. We've created a methodology that you can work with from Day 1, and we'll give you the tools you need to diagnose your UE and help her change. And though we can't anticipate everything you're going to face, and can't give you a quick fix, or cookie-cutter approach, we *will* give you a set of skills that allows you to deal with whatever happens.

This book is a road map. It will guide you from the moment you realize something has to be done, through every step of the way until your unmanageable situation is resolved—either because your UE is far down the road to recovery, or because he's on his way out the door. At that point, you'll have gained closure, a better-functioning team, and the satisfaction of knowing that you can meet the toughest of challenges.

Is it easy? Heck, no!

Is it worth it? YES!

1

Are Unmanageables Made or Born?

Pretty loaded question, right? When your unmanageable is busily turning your office, your team, and maybe your entire life into a total shambles, the easiest thing in the world is to think that she was *born like that*. Born thoughtless. Born clueless. Born unmanageable.

Unless you're one of those admirable people who never permit themselves a judgmental thought, you've probably already found yourself thinking "*She's not a good worker,*" "*He's totally incompetent,*" "*She's an idiot,*" or "*He's selfish.*" And the kicker: "*He'll never change!*" It would be surprising if you didn't occasionally think something along those lines, because those are the things that appear to be true. After all, she's not working well. He is acting incompetently. Her behavior has been idiotic at times. And if he's ever once thought first about the team instead of just about himself, he managed to keep it a secret.

In Anne's executive coaching practice, every manage[illegible] has some complaint about an unruly employee. (The shoe [illegible] the other foot: Jezra coaches many employees who are strugg[illegible]o communicate with their unruly managers!) The cost of all this commotion can be high. Anne estimates that her executive clients lose, on average, 30 percent of their productivity because of issues related to unmanageable employees.

However, there is hope. That hope springs from the fact that there's a world of difference between someone who's *acting* unmanageable, and someone who *can't act any other way*. There's a world of difference between someone who's become unmanageable in response to a particular set of circumstances (that can, at least theoretically, be changed) and someone who's *just like that*.

Of course, the trick is telling the difference. But as you already know, our belief—supported by years of front-line coaching and consulting—is that *most unmanageables can change*. Most of the employees who torment your days (and sometimes sneak into your dreams at night) have the temporary kind of unmanageability. They are, in a word, salvageable. In fact, if the phrase wasn't so unwieldy, we would probably call them "seemingly unmanageable employees," to help you remind yourself that your UE has at least the potential to do better.

Tales From the Trenches

As a management consultant (Anne) and a communications coach (Jezra), we're often contacted by managers who are at the end of their ropes with a UE. These managers are often so exhausted, demoralized, and frustrated by the time they reach us that they see no potential for good in their unmanageables. One example was Anne's client Li. As the executive director of a high-profile, national non-profit organization, his job was to make sure that all the organization's stakeholders—including donors, staff, clients, the community, and media—were happy. *Everybody* had to be happy with the performance of this non-profit; but Li wasn't happy, and it was all due to his #2, Phillipe.

◇◇

Are Unmanageables Made or Born?

According to Li, Philippe was the least self-aware person in the universe. He didn't know how to manage his emotions and didn't understand the impact that his actions had on other people. A private man who covered his own insecurities by yelling at others, Philippe was a walking example of the cliché "failure to communicate." When Li brought Anne in to work on this problem, he was pretty much at his wit's end. "You're a good coach," he told her, "but this isn't going to go anywhere. Philippe's had coaching before, and he didn't get any better. I'm just covering my butt with HR so that, when this fails, too, I can let Philippe go."

Another example of a manager at her wit's end was Sue, who consulted with Anne about how to handle her UE, Daphne. Daphne was a mid-level PR exec whose clients were mostly politicians. Her job was to understand their positions, express them in clear, forceful language, and communicate them to the voters at home. It sounded simple and even exciting, but Daphne couldn't keep anything straight! She confused things like which politician supported which piece of legislation, which message was pro versus con on an issue, and even which state elected which of her clients. Was Daphne intellectually challenged? Hardly! She was an Ivy League graduate who'd broken into the competitive PR field on the strength of her top-notch writing skills. But none of that mattered to Sue anymore, because Sue—like Phillipe's manager, Li—had long since given up on her UE, and just wanted Anne to agree that things were hopeless.

In a third case, Rudy hired Anne to help when he was close to writing off his UE. Celia was a mid-level manager who, after years of B-plus performance, suddenly wasn't achieving her goals, wasn't meeting her deadlines, didn't run effective meetings, and couldn't seem to hold her team accountable. "I know Celia likes her job," Rudy said, "but I can't protect her anymore. She's got to measure up, or leave." In Celia's case, the problem seemed to be an upset in her personal life, which had led to a downward spiral that included sleepless nights, groggy days, lethargy, binge eating, and a low level of job performance that she didn't seem able to change. Like Li and Sue, Rudy didn't believe it was possible to change his totally unmanageable scenario.

Name the Real Problem

When Anne first starts to work with new clients, she always asks them to set five goals. Often, in the beginning, there's no mention of an unmanageable. But (funny thing!) over time, that tends to change.

For instance, Rudy (Celia's manager) started out by saying that one of his goals was to empower and develop his team. As part of their work toward that goal, Anne kept asking Rudy questions about where his team *needed* developing: Who were Rudy's strong performers? Who were the people that didn't deliver? What was going well for his team? And, finally, what was going poorly? (Probing questions are also key to salvaging your unmanageable, as you'll see later in this book.) As he thought about these questions, it didn't take long for Rudy to figure out that what he really meant by *develop my team* was *figure out what to do about Celia!* Until he sat down and thought it through, though, Rudy hadn't quite realized how much of his time Celia was wasting—or how angry he was about it.

Once it surfaced, Rudy's anger got even worse. "I can't believe how much time we spend talking about Celia," he railed almost every week when he spoke with Anne. "I'm losing sleep over this. She's driving me crazy!" This isn't the only time we've heard that comment! It would be ironic if it weren't so sobering: We're in the toughest, most competitive business environment in generations, and what are managers losing sleep over? *How to handle their unruly employees!*

The impact of these situations is huge, and managers can't stop talking about them. Having an unmanageable direct report is like having a pebble in your shoe (when it's not like having your head in a vice). It itches. It rubs. It wears down your sense of perspective. Pretty soon, that little pebble has gone from being an irritation to a major deficit. You're limping, you're weakened, and you don't know how you're going to make it to wherever it was you thought you were going.

In spite of all that—and in spite of the anguish unmanageable employees cause—we're constantly amazed that most of the managers we

◇◇

Are Unmanageables Made or Born?

You Have Reactions, Too!

It's easy to be angry at an unmanageable. They waste your time and that of other team members. They may treat you and others in a thoughtless or infuriating way. They muddy the waters, make extra work, stress everyone's resources, and create problems. It's hard to like an unmanageable, but if you find yourself becoming convinced that he could never have the slightest redeeming good quality, find a way to deal with your own feelings before you try to manage his.

work with are willing to give their UEs one more chance. And the good news is, you don't have to like an unmanageable employee in order to help turn him around. All you need to care about is *his performance*, and the rest will follow.

Take Li, the non-profit manager whose #2, Phillipe, didn't know how to communicate. Although Li considered Philippe a lost cause, he was willing to let Anne try working with him. To Li's surprise, Phillipe rose to the challenge and, in time, began to show improvement. He eventually turned into the right-hand man that Li needed, and, though Li and Phillipe will never be best friends, that isn't such a big deal now that Philippe is an asset to his organization.

Look Below the Surface

One of the things that allowed Li to hold on while Philippe was being transformed was that Li himself was also growing. At first, it was hard for him to imagine that he (or even his organization) might have played any part in Philippe's unmanageability. In time, though, Li came to realize that organizations are like ecosystems: Everything impacts everything else. For example, Philippe's coaching with Anne revealed that the organization's priorities weren't 100-percent clear. Philippe asked Li to create a strategic plan that would help crystallize the goals for their team, and each person's role in achieving them. When Li did so, he noticed that everyone, not just Phillippe, began spending more time on the tasks they now knew were most important. As goals and roles became more transparent, the entire team started working more effectively.

That kind of insight is only possible when you're able to look beneath the surface and see your unmanageable employee as more than the sum of his symptoms. Most of the managers we work with are focused at the symptom level. They don't come in saying *"My UE is a worthless blankety-blank"* (even though that may be what they're thinking). Instead, they give us descriptions of symptoms, such as *"She's become unreliable," "He's never once stepped up to the plate," "She resists every new assignment,"* or *"He constantly complains about things."* There are two things to notice about those statements. First, they're a huge step up from dismissive and blaming comments. And second, they're descriptive, not analytical. They report the surface behavior, but not what's going on beneath.

Anne's response is almost always, "What do you think is going on with your UE *underneath* his unreliability? (or her reticence? or his resistance? or her complaints?)" This question encourages the manager to think more deeply about his UE, and to make observations such as *"She seems distracted and disinterested," "Maybe he doesn't realize what needs to get done," "I get the feeling she's scared to try something new,"* or *"I don't know what's bothering him. I've asked, and he just grunts at me."*

After more discussion and prodding, Anne's clients are able to look even deeper into the possible root causes for their employees' unmanageable behaviors. They might say, *"I think she's losing motivation because she's been so frustrated with her job,"* or *"He doesn't really seem to understand his role on the team,"* or *"She doesn't have much self-confidence,"* or *"I wonder if he's having problems at home."* And now we're getting someplace! Because, unlike complaints or symptom descriptions, these kinds of insights are *actionable*. If you believe that chronic job frustration is prompting your UE's behavior, then that frustration can be reduced, and sometimes even eliminated. An employee's role on the team can be explained. Communications can be improved. And there are numerous ways to help an employee who's in personal crisis cope more effectively on the job.

Seeing beneath the surface takes work. Most of us tend to accept other people's actions and words at face value, so depending on what's going on, you may find it hard to see beyond the obvious. But the effort is well worth it, because looking below the surface (and behind the symptoms your UE presents) will give you a real head start in finding workable solutions.

Watch Out for Early Warning Signs

It's clear that, along with the personal stresses we all face in our daily lives, workplace stress can contribute to an employee becoming unmanageable. We've compiled a list of common job-related stressors, along with examples of the kinds of comments that should alert you to their presence. If you hear statements such as those that follow from your employees, be sure to take them seriously. They are your first clues that trouble may be brewing.

Diminished Motivation

Frustration with a job can grow out of unmet or unrealistic expectations, company-wide uncertainty (rounds of lay-offs are particularly devastating), or relationship problems on a team or with a manager, among many other possible causes. Whether it's gradual or instantaneous, chronic or calamitous, frustration in these areas can sap an employee's motivation—the motivation that might otherwise drive high performance. As a manager, you'll hear the sound of employee frustration in comments such as:

- *"I'm just not into it anymore."*
- *"This job isn't what I expected."*
- *"I can't stand the people on my team."*

Unclear Expectations

It's very easy, and very common, to misunderstand what another person wants, needs, or expects from you. The types of things people miscommunicate about on the job include deadlines, performance expectations, team or project goals, and behavioral *do's* and *don'ts* that grow out of an organization's culture. The instructions given by managers are often not as clear as they would like to think; and employees, for their part, can be slow to ask for clarifications that would save everyone time and effort. Finally, sadly, managers and executives sometimes purposefully lead employees astray, confuse them, or keep them in the dark to avoid unpleasant issues or consolidate power in their own hands. Whatever the source of the confusion, fallout from unclear expectations is often expressed in employee comments such as these:

» *"I have no idea what she wants!"*
» *"It's impossible to satisfy him."*
» *"She thinks everything I do is wrong."*

Lack of Confidence or Self-Esteem

Most people have had the experience of balking over a new responsibility. It's natural to wonder if you have what it takes when the stakes go up or your job becomes more complex. But if that lack of self-confidence persists, an employee can become resistant, defensive, and ultimately unmanageable. An employee who generally doesn't speak up, doesn't take initiative, and isn't rising to the next level may express his dissatisfaction by saying things such as:

» *"I don't know why they thought I could do this!"*
» *"It's just never going to get done."*
» *"Maybe I should switch careers."*

Personal Issues

When your employee is distracted, self-absorbed, or unable to focus, her problem may stem from conditions outside of work. The stress of illness, relationship problems, concerns about children or elderly parents, financial pressures, and much more can show up as negative workplace attitudes and lead to unmanageable acting out. Listen for tell-tale comments such as:

» *"I haven't slept through the night in weeks."*
» *"I just can't seem to concentrate."*
» *"Life is too damned hard these days."*

Are Unmanageables Made or Born?

Watch Out for Behavior Changes

People are definitely unpredictable, but most of us are unpredictable within a fairly narrow behavioral range. The Drama Queen in your department may sometimes tell an ordinary story, and the Snappy Dresser may sometimes wear khakis, but these things aren't totally out of character. It's when she stops talking altogether, or he starts looking like he slept in his clothes, that you should take a closer look. A radical shift in behavior may be your first indication that a good employee is morphing into a UE.

The 11 Unmanageables You'll Meet in This Book

It's easy to see how attitude killers like personal stress, low self-esteem, unmet expectations, and job frustration might trigger unmanageable behaviors in some. But just like with cold germs (which cause headaches in one person, sniffles in another, and chills in the third), there's no real way to predict in advance how an employee will act when her attitude gets "infected." Your best bet is to watch carefully for warning signs (like the comments in the previous section), and move into action as soon as you see them.

And once again, don't be confused or discouraged if your unmanageable is not acting exactly like the UEs that are described in this book. UEs come in a thousand variations, and our goal is not to categorize each one, but to give you a way to analyze and strategize that works *no matter how your UE behaves*. So instead of viewing the UEs that follow as the gold standard of unmanageability, think of them as examples to learn from. That way, you will be prepared to deal with *any* unmanageable employee you face.

The Excuse-Maker

All UEs can be frustrating, but The Excuse-Maker is particularly challenging because nothing is ever her fault. From missed deadlines to half-baked work, it's always due to bad instructions or lazy colleagues or faulty equipment or not enough time. This UE is willing to blame colleagues, clients, even you for her mistakes. It wouldn't surprise you if The Excuse-Maker came in one day and told you that the dog ate her homework.

In **Chapter 3**, you'll learn how to assess your UE's potential value to your team. And because committing to a UE salvage operation is the first step in turning unmanageable behavior around, we'll introduce **The "What's it Worth?" Worksheet.** This worksheet will help you analyze the costs of any type of UE behavior, and the relative costs and benefits of retaining an unmanageable, or letting her go.

The Grumbler

No manager wants to cope with a Grumbler. These "nattering nabobs of negativity" (a phrase coined by political speechwriter William Safire) bring everyone down. Even when they don't manage to squelch your team's every good idea, the steady drip-drip-drip of their complaints can kill an entire team's enthusiasm.

Chapter 4 will show you how to tame a UE who constantly complains by setting behavioral boundaries and helping him relate better to his teammates. You'll also learn about **The Trade-Off Tool,** which can improve work relationships in general, and will help you negotiate behavior change with any kind of UE, at any stage of the salvage process.

The Egomaniac

Me me me me me me me. This UE takes the phrase "not a team player" to new heights. A healthy ego can be a good thing, but the same ego that drives an Egomaniac to succeed can drive her colleagues to distraction. And lately, you've begun to suspect that The Egomaniac doesn't just think about herself all the time; she's actually out for herself all the time, too.

Most people like to believe that their intentions are good, and that other people see their good intentions through the way they act. This is rarely the case with self-absorbed UEs like The Egomaniac. In **Chapter 5,** you'll learn how to hold a mirror up to UEs like The Egomaniac, and create significant change by showing them how other people view their behavior.

◇◇

Are Unmanageables Made or Born?

The Loose Cannon

The Loose Cannon just won't get with the program. He knows what's best for the organization, and isn't interested in being told differently. The fact that he's often a superstar performer makes it even more difficult to rein him in. How do you manage a UE who spends all his time loudly disagreeing with and challenging the organization's goals?

Chapter 6 introduces the important topic of goals clarification. You'll learn to use **The Goals Diagnostic Chart** to define, communicate, create buy-in for, and document the goals of individuals on your team. And when there's confusion about goals—individual, team-based, or throughout your organization—you'll learn how to clarify them so your team can succeed.

The Joker

There's an old expression that says "Laugh and the world laughs with you." But your clients don't think The Joker is funny—they think his attitude is cavalier, because he doesn't seem to take them or their problems seriously. The Joker may be one of your best employees, but if he starts driving clients away, that won't be a laughing matter!

In **Chapter 7**, you'll learn how to manage UEs who have become unruly because they don't understand their *real* role on the team. If an employee is confused about his role, he can't function at the top of his game, and this chapter will show you how to use **The Roles Diagnostic Chart** to analyze and solve that problem.

The Do-Gooder

The Do-Gooder is so busy taking care of everyone else's needs and problems that she hasn't got much time left for that "little detail" known as her own work. And it's hard to discipline her because, not only does everyone love her, but the role she's fulfilling—cheerleader, friendly ear, keeper of the group's morale, bringer of cupcakes—is also necessary for the team's success. Building on the insights from **Chapter 7, Chapter 8** looks at how you can help your UE balance various roles, so that she doesn't ignore the things she *should* be doing in favor of the things she likes to do more.

The Wallflower

Is your invisible shrinking UE shy, or just unwilling to take responsibility? He huddles in his cubicle, won't mix with team members, never volunteers for anything, and won't confront either people or problems. You know The Wallflower has potential, but he won't contribute unless you pry him out of his corner and help him build up his self-confidence.

Not all unmanageables put their problems in your face. A UE who can't perform his job because of shyness or reticence is also a detriment to your team. **Chapter 9** shows you how to capture the talents of Wallflowers and other withdrawn or self-doubting UEs without having to do a personality transplant—simply by observing their efforts, and catching them doing things right.

The Gossip

When it comes to sowing the seeds of discontent, The Gossip knows every trick in the book. Not only does she waste time and effort trash-talking everyone on your team, she seems to have a knack for spreading exactly the kinds of rumors and comments that are most likely to fracture harmony and create tension—particularly when she starts gossiping about the C-Suite.

Questions are key to salvaging any UE. In **Chapter 10**, you'll learn how to de-fang UEs like The Gossip by asking questions that prompt them to re-examine the impact (and advisability) of their unmanageable behavior. As a bonus, you'll also find that becoming adept at asking the right questions makes you a far better manager for *everyone* on your team, not just the UE.

The Slacker

Ho-hum, you want me to work? The Slacker just can't be bothered. Though he may not actually be *lazy (and may even have done good work in the past), you can't help but notice that, lately, he's been phoning in every assignment (and he doesn't even telecommute)! There may be a place for doing the bare minimum, but it's certainly not at the office.*

◇◇

Are Unmanageables Made or Born?

You've worked hard, and your UE has made tremendous strides. Now it's time to lock in those gains and hold even the most hard-core UEs accountable. **The Accountability Tracking Tool**, which you'll learn to use in **Chapter 11,** lets you and your UE agree on benchmarks, monitor progress, and stay focused on high performance for as long as UE salvage takes.

The Rude-nik

When The Rude-nik went from being assertive to being downright rude, her manager tried to convince himself that she was having a bout of artistic temperament. But after The Rude-nik called one colleague a "little twerp," told another she was "useless and stupid," repeatedly interrupted a third, and told her manager to get out of her face, he was done kidding himself!

The Accountability Tracking Tool that you learned about in Chapter 11 isn't just for monitoring hard deliverables. **Chapter 12** will show you how to use this tool to create accountability for soft skills and interpersonal behaviors such as how your UE treats her colleagues, customers, and manager (you!).

The AWOL

If your UE is often late, disappears, no-shows, or "just" neglects an important duty, he's an AWOL. Typically, when someone goes AWOL, his work piles up, deadlines are missed, and important messages go unanswered. And the AWOL creates constant low-grade tension, because everyone knows that somebody's going to have to cover for him, yet again.

Sometimes, in spite of your best efforts, there is no choice but to let a UE go. Recognizing and coping with this decision can be a major challenge for managers, at both the emotional and tactical levels. In **Chapter 13**, you'll learn what to do when all else fails, and how to pick your team up and move on.

The 5 Cs

In addition to the chapters about UEs, **Chapter 2** introduces you to the process that's at the heart of this book. **The 5 Cs** framework will show you how to work with *any* UE, whether or not you find him or her in this book, by applying our foundational steps. This practical and flexible model will help you stay cool and calm under fire, and will give you tools, techniques, and tips that you can apply in any situation to build a strong foundation for success.

Appendices

Unmanageable behaviors can sometimes be caused by generational differences. **Appendix A** provides state-of-the-art thinking about generational differences at work. Knowing the different styles of Baby Boomers, Generation X, and Generation Y can help you speak to them more clearly, manage them more effectively, and make your life (and theirs!) much easier. This chapter will show you how.

Appendix B will also make life easier, because it contains all the forms and "cheat sheets" discussed in **Chapters 3** through **13**. Copy them. Work with them. Adapt them to your own needs. These tools will help you salvage unmanageable situations, and UEs.

Learning to Love Your UE

If you've been managing people for any length of time, the chances are pretty good that you've already met (and struggled with) a few unmanageable employees. Whether your experience was good, bad, or indifferent—whether your UE reformed, retired, or was shown the door—this book, and the model it presents, will help you *succeed* with UEs in the future. We will show you how to:

» *Diagnose unmanageable employee behaviors.*
» *Create the right approach and action plan for each individual situation.*
» *Apply proven techniques and tools to help your UE become a productive and full participant at work.*

Best of all, you will stop blaming and start changing the UE who's made your job so difficult. And you'll reap the rewards of managing a team in which everyone is pointed toward success.

Are you ready to begin?

◇◇

Are Unmanageables Made or Born?

2

The 5 Cs

Inanimate objects are relatively easy to manage. If your house is cold, you turn up the heat. If your heater is broken, you put on a sweater—and then get the heater fixed or replaced. But people are almost never that simple. Multi-layered problems aren't the exception in business; they're the rule. That's why managers need a multi-layered process to cope with the complex demands of handling both a UE *and* their regular jobs!

The process that we recommend (and that you'll learn about throughout this book) has five steps that will take you through observing, evaluating, diagnosing, communicating about, and finally resolving your UE challenges. This objective and comprehensive framework will guide you from beginning to end—or, from admitting there's a problem to deciding how to handle it, to putting your plan into action, to dealing with push-back, and to monitoring success.

That may sound like a lot of work, and sometimes it is. But if you think dealing with an unmanageable employee is hard work, just try *not* dealing with him. In terms of time, money, attention, and emotion, a UE who's running wild can wreak unbelievable havoc. Cleaning up the mess he leaves behind—now *that's* hard work!

The 5 Cs Are Your One-Stop Solution

Okay, you understand our premise that most UEs can be saved. (To avoid religious overtones, we'll call that "salvaged" from now on.) So now what? Here is the five-step methodology that will guide you to the best possible solution:

1. *Commit or Quit*
2. *Communicate*
3. *Clarify Goals and Roles*
4. *Coach*
5. *Create Accountability*

For obvious reasons, we call these steps **The 5 Cs**. When used comprehensively and in this order, they add up to an approach that will let you cope with anything a UE throws at you. Following this method will guarántee that your thinking (and your actions) are clear, consistent, and well-organized, and that you have the best possible chance of success.

Each one of **The 5 Cs** is foundational—which means that each step supports the next. Skipping even one of the steps may leave you without vital information, so always work **The 5 Cs** from beginning to end. You may not need to spend equal or lengthy amounts of time on every step, but you will need to at least touch on each of them in order to get the best results.

Step 1: Commit or Quit

The first choice a manager faces, with any UE, is the choice of *whether to try to retain the UE or not*. This is a matter that requires careful thinking. After all, you're weighing the costs and benefits of taking on a major challenge (UE salvage) against the costs and benefits of starting from scratch by finding and hiring a new employee.

This decision is a significant one, because UE salvage, if you decide to attempt it, requires that you make a firm and serious commitment to your unmanageable employee's future.

What!? you may be thinking. *Commit to her? How about 'tolerate' her; isn't that enough? Can't I just try a few helpful things and see if she gets better?* Unfortunately, the answer is no, and here's why: If you don't care about your UE, and don't commit to her professional success, she's going to know that, and she'll resist any help that you offer. Here's why:

Imagine that someone who's really important to you is having a bad problem—a nasty divorce, a bout with cancer, a car accident, an eating disorder. Do you think, "*Okay, I'll try a few helpful things, and see if he gets better?*" Probably not. If you truly care about this person, you'll probably be committed to doing whatever it takes to help him turn his life around, and a UE salvage operation requires no less. People find it easier to change when they know that the person who's pushing for change cares about them; and your UE is no exception.

We'll be honest: You may not like your UE, and you don't have to. But if you have any thought of trying to bring this employee around to being an asset, you *will* have to find a way to commit yourself to her professional growth and success. And by the way, even if you commit to your UE in the beginning, you'll be reaffirming that choice every step along the way. You may find, for example, that your UE agrees there's a problem, but won't work with you to solve it. Or that he's willing to work with you, but not to accept accountability. At every step of **The 5 Cs**, you *and* the UE must tacitly re-commit to success.

Of course, once you've used **The 5 Cs** to turn your UE around, you may start spontaneously feeling better about her (or at least, her performance). Does that mean that you two will start hanging out and watching football together? Probably not. But frustrations will gradually ease, and your entire team will feel the benefits that come from a lowered level of tension.

In the next chapter, you'll learn how to use an objective decision-making tool called **The "What's it Worth?" Worksheet** to quantify your UE problem, estimate the cost of creating a solution, and compare the cost of that solution with the costs of letting your UE go.

The worksheet also includes your subjective evaluation of the UE's potential. Quantifying things that *can* be quantified, and taking note of the things that can't, will give you a comprehensive and dispassionate way to examine your options with confidence. In **Chapter 3**, we'll take you step by step through how to use **The "What's it Worth?" Worksheet**, and show you how to achieve clarity about whether to commit to your UE, or quit trying.

Step 2: Communicate

Assuming that you've committed to working with your UE, you are now engaged in a UE salvage operation. Your next step is one that many managers try hard to avoid: a frank and open conversation with the person who's been making your life hell.

Don't worry, though; you won't be winging it. Armed with the information that you collected during **Step 1**, you will start by presenting your view of the problem, including information about its impact, to your unmanageable. Ideally, the UE would agree with your view, but if he doesn't, you'll at least walk away knowing how his understanding of the problem differs from yours. Through ongoing communication, you two *can* ultimately agree on a definition of the problem and on how you'll work together to solve it—and we'll show you how to reach that agreement.

One of your tools will be **The 10 Communications Questions**. (**The 10 Communications Questions** are also available in **Appendix B**, along with all the other tools in this book.) These questions will help you prepare for your first encounter with the UE, and will also show you where you need to do more, or better, thinking to succeed.

The 10 Communications Questions
1. What problem is my UE presenting?
2. Do I have any sense of the root cause of the problem?
3. What's the impact on my UE's performance?

The 10 Communications Questions
4. What's the impact on my team?
5. What actions have I taken so far?
6. How has my UE responded to those actions?
7. When will I hold a conversation with my UE?
8. What are the main points I want to get across?
9. What are the questions I might ask my UE?
10. How will I know if the talk is a success?

As you can see, good planning is the key to success in **Step 2.** Before you talk to your UE, be sure you know your goal for the conversation and what details you plan to cover. Then, when the time comes, you'll be able to stay with the program and not get pulled into any off-topic details, emotions, or even accusations from your UE.

In addition to setting your goals for **Step 2**, you'll find it useful to set some ground rules when you and your UE sit down to talk. Be sure that, before the conversation starts, *you both agree* to handle things with:

» *RESPECT: Speak politely; no raised voices.*
» *COURTESY: Take turns; wait for the other to finish.*
» *NEUTRALITY: Report the facts; don't demean what the other person says. Instead of shouting, "You're wrong!" try saying, "You and I disagree about that." Instead of sneering, "Yeah, right!" try saying, "I'm finding that hard to believe."*
» *RESPONSIBILITY: Talk about yourself, not the other person. Instead of "You're driving me crazy," try saying, "I was upset when X happened." Instead of "What could you possibly have been thinking?" try saying, "I don't understand your motives."*

» *CONFIDENTIALITY: If either of you gossips about this conversation, you've lost your chance at mutual trust. It's fine to give a general report ("We talked about how to make things better"), but don't quote details or tell stories.*

Step 2: Communicate may take one or several conversation. By the end of this step, though, you and your UE should generally agree that there is a problem, that the problem is damaging your team, and that you're going to work together to solve it. Now it's time to dig below the surface, and start deciding *how* that change will happen.

Step 3: Clarify Goals and Roles

Most people believe that they know what's expected of them at work. But problems arise when employees "know" things that aren't true—and become frustrated when what they "know" should be happening, isn't. That's why, as you and your UE discuss her behavior, you may discover that some of it stems from a misunderstanding of where (and how) she fits into the organization. Often, this lack of clarity revolves around the UE's **goals** (what she is expected to accomplish as an employee), and/or her **role** (how she is expected to function within the team; what responsibilities are hers, and not hers).

Know Your Ultimate Destination

Anne works with the Defense Intelligence Agency, where she often hears it said that if you start out just one degree off course, you could end up totally missing your target. And the farther you have to travel, the worse this situation will get. (If you're one degree off and going one mile, you'll wind up a lot closer than if you're one degree off and heading toward the moon!) The same thing is true in business: If your UE's understanding of her goals and role are even a small amount off course, your entire team can miss its target.

Goals

Everyone wants to know what they are supposed to be doing at work. Otherwise, they feel rudderless and without a purpose. It's disconcerting to be misaligned with your colleague or team, and it can lead to a negative cascade of misunderstandings, misspent energy, frustration, and, finally, "unmanageability." Clarifying expectations in this area sometimes results in lessened frustration, which can, in turn, lead to improved behavior.

To prevent this negative cascade, *every* employee must be clear about the goals they are expected to achieve. But those goals can't be arbitrary, nebulous, or beyond reach. To be effective, goals must share key characteristics, no matter the nature of your organization. They must be outcome-oriented; purposeful (they have to answer the questions *"so what?"* or *"who cares?"* and be of clear value to your employees); and SMART (specific, measurable, agreed-upon, relevant, and time-based). In **Chapter 6**, you'll learn more about each of these criteria. You'll also discover how to establish and assign clear goals, and get buy-in from your team members.

Roles

Just as every organization and team has goals that need to be clearly understood, each person on your team has both *formal* and *informal* roles that need to be clearly understood. A **role** comprises the set of actions that each employee is responsible for carrying out. Often these overlap with a person's title or job description, but surprisingly often, they don't.

Formal roles are the ones that you see on an organizational chart. **Informal roles** are generally held by "influencers"—people who may not have organizational authority, but who everyone respects and listens to. These people might be night supervisors, secretaries, or people who no longer work for the organization. Their title (if they even have one) may be irrelevant; what counts is the influence they're able to wield. In **Chapter 7**, we'll show you how to clarify any employee's workplace roles. And in **Chapter 8**, you'll learn how to help your employees balance the amount of energy they give to each role. (Taking too little *and* too much responsibility can create problems.)

Step 4: Coach

At the heart of many UEs' behavior is a problem with their **attitude**. We define attitude as *the inner focus and motivation that a person brings to the activities in his or her life*. Although some UEs will self-correct following a frank communication (or when you've clarified their **roles** and **goals**), most will need to examine and shift the inner attitudes that are giving rise to unmanageability.

You're just the person to coach your UE through that—yet many managers are wary of coaching. They don't believe in getting into people's heads. Or they feel overburdened, and see coaching as another skill set that they don't have the time or energy to learn.

Fortunately, coaching can be quickly learned, and even more quickly applied to UEs. It's one of your most powerful and flexible tools. And that's good, because in most unmanageable situations, your UE will eventually require some amount of coaching—by you!

What Is the Coaching Process?

A coach is not a therapist, a cheerleader, or a New Age guru. A coach is someone who *helps people find their own solutions by asking questions*. Of course, not just any question will do. As a manager who sometimes takes on the added role of coach, you will learn to ask questions that help your employees think through their own behavioral problems, find their own solutions to those problems, and develop the motivation to change in a positive way.

Why do they need to find the solution? One reason is buy-in: People are more likely to invest in solutions that they discover for themselves. Another reason is that—and this is a tough lesson for many managers to learn—*you can't know the answer to every problem*, particularly the ones in other people's minds! For example:

Sarah and Raul are working on a major sales software implementation project for your company. As your top salesperson, Sarah is the team's "content expert," and Raul is the project programmer. Although Sarah and Raul got off to a strong start, and although Raul has always been a hard-working employee, Sarah now feels that he isn't pulling his weight on the team. He often leaves critical work unfinished at the day's end; he isn't working the hours Sarah believes are warranted; and he bristles when she pressures him to do more.

There is only one person who can answer the question *"What's causing Raul to act like this?"* That person is Raul himself—and coaching is the way to get that question asked and answered.

Before Deciding to Coach a UE

In her book *A Manager's Guide to Coaching*, Anne and her coauthor Brian Emerson discuss the following equation for success:

aptitude + attitude + available resource = level of success

The idea is that, to succeed in any work-related task, an employee must apply a combination of relevant skills (aptitude), motivation (attitude), and time, money, equipment, help, and so on (available resources). Using the example of Sarah and Raul, here's how to use this equation to start diagnosing Raul's problem:

- *If Raul lacks* **aptitude***—the basic skills needed to implement the new software—your job as his manager is to provide training.*
- *If Raul lacks* **available resources***—for instance, an adequate computer system—your job is to get him what he needs.*
- *If Raul lacks neither of those things, the only variable left to explain why he isn't doing a good job is* **attitude**.
- *Knowing that attitude is probably at the root of Raul's problem, you have two choices: You can take a* **directive approach***, saying something like, "Raul, I expect you to give more time to this project. I'm canceling your vacation, and unless your performance improves, you'll be fired." Or you can*

> *take a* **coaching approach***, asking questions that lead to insights that improve Raul's motivation, so that he decides to give more to the project. (Of course, you know which approach we're going to recommend!)*

Your Five-Minute Coaching Primer

When we tell our clients about coaching, a common push-back we hear is *"I'm already* way *too busy. I don't have time for that."* There are three things wrong with this reasoning: First, coaching will actually save you time in the long run—the time it takes to deal with your unmanageable situation! Second, coaching doesn't take much time; a good coaching conversation can literally be a few sentences long. And third, you can become a good coach *fast*; it only takes a few minutes to learn how.

So here it is, in just a few minutes (and you'll learn more in **Chapter 10**): The centerpiece of effective coaching is the ability to ask good coaching questions. Questions are also your best approach because, many times, your UE doesn't know why he's acting so badly. He probably doesn't know the answer, and could use your help in figuring it out. Your interested, non-judgmental, open-ended questions give him an opportunity to think about what's going on, and may even spark him to make changes without you having to ask. Questions that are most likely to produce that result have these three qualities in common:

1. **They are open-ended**. **Closed questions** *can be answered with a single word, such as* "Can you do this?" *or* "Will you be finished today?", *and tend to shut down discussion and dialogue.* **Open-ended questions** *start with words such as what, where, and how (but not why): "What are the possibilities, here?" or "How will you know when it's done?" Questions like these draw out your UE and create a space for thought and conversation.*

2. **They are advice-free**. *Most people find "questions" such as "Have you thought of X?" or "Why don't you try Y?" annoying, because they're not really questions at all—they're statements (advice) that end with question marks. Real coaching questions aren't thinly disguised opinions; they're neutral, and they reflect the questioner's interest in learning something she doesn't know.*
3. **They are concise**. *Powerful questions usually contain eight words or less: "What does that look like?," "What will you do next?," or "Where will you be in five years?" are all examples of effective, open-ended, advice-free, thought-provoking, and forward-focused questions that are concise and to the point.*

Good coaching questions avoid any hint of blame, because blame makes people defensive and uncooperative—the opposite of your desired effect. So no matter how badly you've been provoked, don't let yourself hit back with blaming questions such as *"What's wrong with you?"* or *"Why is your work so bad?"*

Good at Work, Good at Home

Good coaching questions aren't just effective at work; they can also be useful in private conversations. Even in a personal context, most of us would prefer to be asked a neutral, curious question than told ("for our own good") what's wrong with us. Imagine the following scenarios. Which approach do you think will get the best response?

Your best friend says he's quitting his job and doesn't have another one lined up.

» **You tell him:** *"Well, that sounds pretty stupid to me! You'll probably run out of money in about six weeks. I sure hope you know what you're doing, but don't think you're going to sleep on my couch when you're flat broke and have nothing going on in your life!"*

- **You ask him:** *"That's interesting. How will quitting your job change your standard of living?" or "Quitting your job. Hmmm.... What do you want to be doing a year from now?"*

Your spouse says she wants her mother to move in.

- **You tell her:** *"That's ridiculous! You and your mother hate each other. If she moves in here, life is going to be hell for everyone. I won't stand for it!"*
- **You ask her:** *"That sound like it might be a challenge. What's the longest you and your mother have ever gone without getting into a fight?" or "Your mother is good at pushing your buttons. How will you manage your anger if she constantly criticizes you in your own home?"*

The ability to ask good coaching questions is a game-changing skill. Previously, you and your UE worked together to define and clarify her "problem"—but until she begins to own that problem's

Ask, Don't Tell

Most of us are more trusting of answers that we discover for ourselves. How many times have you ignored a truth when you heard it from a well-meaning friend or family member, only to later discover to your "total surprise" that what people were saying had value after all? And how open would you have been to hearing that same insight from your manager? (Probably not very.) Good coaching questions help defuse the natural human tendency to resist other people's insights by letting your UE (or other employee) discover the truth about what's going on for herself. An added benefit to this approach is that you don't have to know all the answers. Remember that, although you may have theories about what is behind your UE's behavior, you can't really know what's going on with her unless she tells you.

solution, her behavior is unlikely to change. Coaching questions make ownership possible, by putting responsibility squarely back in your UE's court, and confronting her with the clear option to choose a new course of action, or not. If she takes responsibility and chooses change, your next area of focus will be to support her effort with **Step 5** of **The 5 Cs: Create Accountability**.

Step 5: Create Accountability

In **Step 1** of **The 5 Cs**, you committed to salvaging your UE. In **Step 2**, you communicated with him about the problem in a frank and effective way. **Step 3** involved clarifying your organization's goals, and his goals and role in achieving them, which eliminated any confusion about what he's supposed to be doing at work. And with **Step 4**, you've coached him to adopt a new attitude. It would be nice if all your work was now done. But unfortunately, transforming a UE is rarely a linear process. Few things in life are permanent, and left to their own devices, most people will begin to backslide almost immediately.

Old behaviors and habits have tremendous power, as anyone who's ever tried to quit smoking or stay on an eating plan will attest. The same is true of attitudes, which may be the hardest habits to break of all. That's why it's mandatory that you help your UE stay on track by creating a system to hold him accountable. Rather than patting your (hopefully former) UE on the back and wishing him good luck as you sail off into your next challenge, put in some serious time and effort to create a system that will help him deliver the changes he's promised to make and the commitments he's promised to meet. The habit of unmanageability can never be rooted out once and for all; the trick is to chop off any new branches before they begin to flower.

Accountability Is a Two-Way Street

Accountability isn't just about your UE being accountable to you. It's also about your commitment to help him succeed by being vigilant in monitoring his progress. That's why it's helpful to think of this as a joint venture. If you and your UE cooperate on determining how to create accountability, there's a much greater chance that *both of you* will fulfill this part of your commitment.

To that end, ask your UE questions such as *"How will I know that things are changing?" "What's the best way for us to check in?" "When will you let me know how it's going?"* and *"How will you tell me if you need more help?"* Ideally, your UE will also be asking similar questions, such as *"What's the best way to quickly run an idea past you?," "Who else can I turn to as a sounding board?,"* and *"Will you give me more time to reach a goal if I need it?"*

The Map Is Not the Territory

As you begin the journey of UE salvage, remember that *no* road map, however detailed and accurate, can fully represent what you'll encounter in real life. **The 5 Cs** lay out a route for guiding your UE from unmangeability back to productivity, but there are bound to be twists and turns along the way—hills and valleys that are unique to your situation. You might pass a landmark without noticing it, or keep circling back around the same closed loop. You might get lost. Or run out of steam. Or wonder why you ever got started. But all those obstacles will fade from view, once you reach your destination.

The journey begins with a simple question: *What's this person worth to my team?* That will be the topic of our next chapter.

3

The Excuse-Maker

There's no question that salvaging your UE is going to be an adventure. So before you undertake this complicated, ongoing process, it's important to decide if you're *truly* committed to seeing it through. Otherwise, you risk wasting your precious time and energy—and, with all the time and energy you've already lost to your UE, losing more is the last thing you need!

How do you make the best decision about whether or not to salvage your UE? In this chapter, we'll show you how to decide by looking at the costs and benefits of working to salvage his potential, or letting him go before things get worse. Going through that process will help you look at your UE problem from every angle, and give you confidence in your choice. The analysis will also help you support your decision, to salvage (or not salvage) your unmanageables to your own higher-ups.

Meet the Excuse-Maker

All UEs can be frustrating, but the Excuse-Maker is particularly challenging because this UE believes that nothing is her fault. Her attitude makes it very difficult for you to talk with her about a problem, and her constant habit of laying blame on other people makes you feel as if the two of you are in a constant, dizzying circle dance of *he said-she said*. What's worse, the dance gets wider and more frantic as time goes on, because the Excuse-Maker keeps pulling more and more people out onto the floor—blaming colleagues, clients, and even you for her own mistakes. It will take clear and detailed planning for you to overcome this UE's fancy footwork.

Case Study: Teflon Jenny

Marcus is the manager of a small team within a large accounting firm. His clients expect quality and attention to detail, and Marcus has always delivered it in record time. Until her performance began to slip, Jenny—whom Marcus had hand-picked for his team—was a trusted part of that effort, but no more! In just the last month, Jenny failed to double-check a client's fixed costs, which created errors in the client's P&L statement, and she blamed this on the client. Then she gave incorrect tax information to another top client, and blamed that on her colleague Luca (who hotly denied it was his fault). She was three weeks late getting Q1 results to another client, and blamed this on the computer system. The client was furious, and Marcus had to offer a $1,000 discount on the client's Q2 invoice in order to save the relationship.

Then came the final straw: Jenny was more than an hour late for a meeting at which she was scheduled to present a client's year-end results—and when she finally arrived, she acted as if nothing unusual had happened. When Marcus confronted her about it later, she shrugged and blamed her lateness on bad traffic. Rather than say something that he might regret, Marcus just turned and stormed out of the room.

Has This Ever Happened to You?

Have you ever wondered how unmanageable employees can push our buttons with such unerring skill? In this case study, Jenny was offending Marcus on two levels—first, through her behavior, and second, through her seeming indifference to the consequences. At the moment when he walked away from her, being objective about Jenny was the last thing Marcus wanted to do.

Keep Your Cool

If your UE is making you crazy enough to say or do something you might regret, immediately leave the room to cool down. It's best if you can make a reasonable statement, such as "We'll talk more about this later," instead of just stalking out the door, but the important thing is to remove yourself from the temptation to act unprofessionally. When you've done that, take a minute to breathe, think, or consult other resources before you take any action, make any decision, or wade back into the fray with your UE.

The ability to recognize your own breaking point, and head off disaster in advance, is one of the skills that make up self-awareness. Self-awareness means that you are aware of your own hot buttons, triggers, and rising emotions, and can act to prevent things from getting out of hand. An unself-aware manager may not feel her own rising tide of emotions and may say or do something regrettable that's driven by pure frustration. A self-aware manager, on the other hand, will notice the frustration and cool down before taking any further action. Remember: However wrong your UE may be from a practical, moral, or manners perspective, it is still your responsibility, as her manager, to be the adult in the room, and to keep your behavior beyond reproach and under control.

After Marcus had calmed down, he decided to speak with his VP of Human Resources. "Jenny won't improve on her own," the VP of HR told Marcus. "I know you don't want to spend more time trying to figure out what to do with her, but you have to commit to a course of action." She then gave him **The "What's it Worth?" Worksheet**, and asked him to keep her in the loop.

Problem

When you try to decide whether to undertake a UE salvage effort or show your unmanageable out the door, you'll quickly discover that *emotion* is no guide. That's because, if you're somewhere between frustrated and furious about the trouble your UE is causing, you'll probably lean heavily toward the chopping block. And *numbers* may not tell the story, because much of what's happening (such as the potential value if your UE can be salvaged) is hard to quantify. You can't even rely on other people's advice, because no one knows the situation like you do.

So how do you sort through all those factors, and come up with a responsible decision? By utilizing **The "What's it Worth?" Worksheet**. (The worksheet, like all the other tools in this book, is available in its full form in **Appendix B**.) The worksheet comprises three robust yet flexible sections that give you varying snapshots of the problem at hand. Taken as a whole, it allows you to evaluate both the tangible and intangible costs and benefits of committing to or quitting your unmanageable.

The "What's it Worth?" Worksheet

Part 1: Cost of the UE's Problem

Estimated Cost of Manager's Time	Hrs./Week	6 Mo. Cost
Time spent with UE		

Estimated Cost of Manager's Time	Hrs./Week	6 Mo. Cost
Time spent with other involved employees		
Time with HR, lawyer, or senior management		
Time managing fall out with clients		
Other		
Total Estimated Cost of Manager's Time		

Estimated Cost of Lost Employee Productivity	Percentage	6 Mo. Cost
Productivity lost by the UE		
Productivity lost by other involved employees		
Other		
Total Estimated Cost of Lost Employee Productivity		

Estimated Direct Costs	Current	6 Mo. Cost
Compensation for product or service mistakes		
Costs of damage to equipment, etc.		
Other		
Total Estimated Costs		

Estimated Opportunity Costs	Current	6 Mo. Cost
Missed deadlines		
Bids not completed		
Projects not developed		
Other		
Total Estimated Opportunity Costs		

As you can see, **Part 1** of the worksheet helps you evaluate the current and projected costs of your problem from varying perspectives. It allows you to describe and, where possible, quantify *the amount that your UE has cost your organization to date*. Although it's difficult to put a number on the cost of ongoing unmanageableness, it's important to try, because that cost might be far less (or far more!) than you think. As anyone who's ever managed a UE knows, there are three types of costs associated with their behavior:

- **Time** *spent on the employee's problems.*
- **Money** *lost due to the UE's actions or inaction.*

- » **Opportunities** *that have been lost or sidetracked because you or your team was focused on the UE.*

But present costs don't tell the whole story. If you allow your unmanageable employee to keep going down her present road, the costs will begin to mount, sometimes exponentially. That's why **Part 1** of the worksheet also looks at the likely costs of your UE's behavior if it continues for six more months. We've chosen the six-month benchmark because, on average, our clients have started to see new behaviors taking root in approximately three months, and fully blooming in approximately six months. (That's if our client is working with the UE on a consistent schedule of at least every other week.) Three to six months is thus a reasonable length of time for executing a UE salvage plan; and conversely, a problem that doesn't improve in that timeframe is unlikely to yield to further efforts.

The Worksheet in Action

As Marcus studied **The "What's it Worth?" Worksheet**, he began to feel more hopeful than he had in months. Finally, he could imagine making an *objective* decision about Jenny's future status with the firm—one that didn't involve yelling, walking away, or having to listen to excuses for her UE behavior. With this in mind, Marcus calculated the following:

- » *The time he'd spent talking to Jenny about her mistakes and listening to her make excuses had increased to two hours per week. During the next six months, that would come to 52 hours, or a full week's work. This shocked Marcus.*
- » *Marcus had spent about 45 minutes that week smoothing Luca's ruffled feathers after Jenny blamed Luca for one of her mistakes. He estimated that this type of smoothing things over would total 20 hours over the next six months.*
- » *His visit to HR had taken 30 minutes—and the VP had asked him to keep in touch, which meant that this item would take up more time in the future. Marcus estimated an hour a month, or approximately .25 hours per week.*

» *Marcus was spending about an hour a week managing clients who were upset with Jenny. If that time grew, he was going to be one very unhappy manager.*

Actually, Marcus was already unhappy. Four hours of the 55 he worked each week, pro-rated at his $75,000 salary, meant that Jenny could burn almost $3,000 of *his time alone* in just six months. The first section of **Part 1** of his worksheet looked like this:

Estimated Cost of Manager's Time	Hrs./Week	6 Mo. Cost
Time spent with UE	2 hrs/wk.	--
Time spent with other involved employees	.75 hrs/wk.	--
Time with HR, lawyer, or senior management	.25 hrs/wk.	--
Time managing fall-out with clients	1 hr/wk.	--
Other	--	--
Total Estimated Cost of Manager's Time	4 hrs/wk.	~$3,000

Time Is Not on Your Side

It's easy to minimize the amount of time you spend on a UE, yet every 10-minute conversation with (or about) the UE adds up. This can become a significant outlay of time that could be used for other things. Track the time you spend on your UE for one week; you may find the results surprising.

◇◇

The Excuse-Maker

Then Marcus began to calculate the next section of **Part 1: Estimated Cost of Lost Employee Productivity.** Because he wasn't able to track other people's hours as closely as his own, this section asked Marcus to estimate the percentage of the time his direct reports were losing due to Jenny's behavior.

- *If he looked just at time, not effectiveness, Jenny was operating at 90% of her usual productivity; over six months, he would lose 5 percent of her $60,000 salary, or $3,000.*
- *Luca would probably lose 5 percent of his productive time if he and Jenny kept butting heads; half a year of that, at Luca's $50,000 annual salary, would be $1,250.*

Over six months, that would be $4,200. Added to the $3,000 of Marcus's time that would potentially be lost, it was mind-boggling—and those numbers were conservative!

Estimated Cost of Lost Employee Productivity	Percentage	6 Mo. Cost
Productivity lost by the UE	10%	$3,000
Productivity lost by other involved employees	5%	$1,250
Other	--	--
Total Estimated Cost of Lost Employee Productivity	--	~$4,200

The next category in **Part 1** is **Direct Costs.** So far, the only direct cost Marcus could ascribe to Jenny was the $1,000 rebate he'd offered a client after Jenny delayed his company's Q1 reports. In the interest of his rapidly rising blood pressure, Marcus decided to skip doing a six-month direct cost projection.

Estimated Direct Costs	Current	6 Mo. Cost
Compensation for product or service mistakes	$1,000	--
Costs of damage to equipment, etc.	--	--
Other	--	--
Total Estimated Direct Costs	$1,000	--

The last section of **Part 1** asks you for **Estimated Opportunity Costs**. Though it's vital to calculate the *actual* costs of your UE's behavior, it's just as important to consider the cost of opportunities that were lost because time and money were used unproductively. Ask yourself: *"What was I not able to accomplish because I was focused on my UE?"* Before tackling this section, Marcus took a few deep breaths and went to fill his coffee mug. Then he jumped in.

- *Because he had already listed the $1,000 client rebate as a compensation cost, Marcus decided to leave it there (it could also have been an item under "missed deadlines").*
- *And though it hurt to admit this, Marcus knew that, because of his attention to Jenny's unmanageability and excuse-making, he had given short shrift to a new marketing campaign that was potentially worth approximately $100,000 per year to the firm. If things continued for another six months, half the projected $100K value of that campaign would be lost for this year, at a cost to the business of $50,000.*

Estimated Opportunity Costs	Current	6 Mo. Cost
Missed deadlines	--	--
Bids not completed	--	--
Projects not developed	--	$50,000
Other	--	--
Total Estimated Opportunity Costs	--	$50,000

At this point, Marcus was looking at a very sobering picture: If Jenny's problems continued at their current level, *she was likely to cost his firm more than $8,200 in employee time and other direct costs, and $50,000 in lost opportunities over the next six months.*

Marcus was ready to pull the plug now! Fortunately, the VP of HR had cautioned him that this would be his first reaction, and insisted that he complete the entire worksheet before making a final decision. So even though he suspected it was just going to confirm his inclination to let Jenny go, Marcus turned to **Part 2** of **The "What's it Worth?" Worksheet**.

Part 2: Estimated Cost of "UE Salvage Operation"

Estimated Cost of "UE Salvage Operation"	Hrs./ Week	6 Mo. Cost
Manager's time		
Internal consultant's time (HR, legal, etc.)		

Estimated Cost of "UE Salvage Operation"	Hrs./ Week	6 Mo. Cost
External consultant evaluation (if desired)		
External coaching (for UE and/or manager)		
Other		
Total estimated cost of "UE Salvage Operation"		
Estimated cost of UE replacement (2–2.5 x annual salary)		

Marcus's first reaction was, *"What? More costs?"* When he considered the matter he realized that of course it would take time and skill to turn Jenny around, and that meant more expense. But this was hardly likely to incline him in her favor. Nevertheless, he tipped his chair back and started filling out **Part 2.**

» *Because Jenny's unmanageability was already taking four hours of his time each week, it seemed like a reasonable plan to devote one additional hour each week to finding and implementing a possible solution. Marcus wrote that number down.*
» *In Marcus's accounting firm, the time of internal consultants from HR or the legal department wasn't billed to other managers, so he left that item blank.*
» *Marcus had thought hard about whether there was a larger problem with his team that might be fueling Jenny's unmanageability. He'd even spoken with a few of the older managers and the VP of HR, but no one thought this was an issue. Because he didn't seem to have an organizational development*

or structural team problem, Marcus decided that bringing in an external consultant would be a bad use of his funds. He left this item blank, too.

» *On the other hand, external coaching for Jenny seemed like a wise investment. Marcus didn't want to be her coach in an ongoing way; he wanted to focus on his team, and business. Marcus estimated that an external executive coach would cost $300–$500 an hour, and would require a minimum of 10 to 12 hour-long coaching sessions for maximum effectiveness; therefore, $5,000 seemed a reasonable amount to budget for this item.*

Marcus was surprised to see that the estimated cost of a six-month salvage operation ($6,700) was less than what it would cost to simply handle Jenny's UE behavior for six months ($8,200). And that was without including the opportunity cost of the distractions she created, which he'd estimated at $50,000. Clearly, pushing for change was preferable to letting the status quo continue.

But what really caught Marcus's attention was the last item in **Part 2** of **The "What's it Worth?" Worksheet.** Like many managers, he was surprised to see that the replacement cost for a mid-level employee seemed very high. In fact, though, these numbers are conservative. The Society for Human Resource Management (SHRM) has noted that it costs *$3,500* to replace an *$8/hour employee*. Other industry sources have estimated that it costs 30 to 50 percent of annual salary to replace an entry-level employee, 150 percent of annual salary to replace a mid-level employee, and up to 400 percent of annual salary to replace specialized, high-level employees!

This shocks many managers. They've always thought that the best thing they could do for their organization would be to shuffle a resource-consuming unmanageable unceremoniously out the door. But that kind of thinking doesn't account for the tremendous costs associated with an employee leaving the organization. These costs include lost productivity as an employee prepares to leave (due to total lack of interest, and those long hours she spends looking for another job on your dime!), exit costs, the costs of recruiting a new employee, hiring costs, orientation and training for the new employee, administrative costs, the productivity lost as the new employee onboards to the demands of his new position, and more.

And that's just for an average employee. When your UE is a superstar, a person of high rank, or someone with special or unique skills, the costs of replacing her can skyrocket. It's no wonder that high performers can often rack up many unmanageable points before things reach a crisis; no one wants to deal with the complex problem of replacing them!

Given the level of Jenny's position, the VP of HR had suggested to Marcus that he use 200 to 250 percent of her annual salary for this exercise. Because her salary was $60,000, the estimated cost of replacing her would be anywhere from $120,000 to $150,000—and there was no guarantee that the new employee would work out better, or provide more value to Marcus's team. When he was done filling out this section of the Worksheet, it looked like this:

Estimated Cost of "UE Salvage Operation"	Hrs./ Week	6 Mo. Cost
Manager's time	1 hrs./ wk	~$700
Internal consultants' time (HR, legal, etc.)	--	--
External consultant evaluation (if desired)	--	--
External coaching (for UE and/or manager)	--	$5,000
Other	--	--
Total estimated cost of "UE Salvage Operation"		$6,700

◇◇

The Excuse-Maker

Estimated Cost of "UE Salvage Operation"	Hrs./ Week	6 Mo. Cost
Estimated Cost of UE Replacement (2–2.5 x annual salary)	$120,000–150,000	

Marcus didn't know what to do now. The numbers pointed toward retaining Jenny, but he didn't really trust her to change, and felt unsure of how to make a final decision. Then he remembered the final piece of the worksheet, **Part 3: Benefits of "UE Salvage."**

Part 3: Benefits of "UE Salvage"

Benefits of "UE Salvage"
Was your UE ever a fully productive employee? If so, what was his/her major contribution?
What would this UE contribute to your team if he/she was functioning fully now?
What incremental benefits from his/her participation might be captured over time?

61

It's tempting to make a **Commit or Quit** decision by looking only at what your UE costs. But you owe it to yourself and your organization to look at the potential benefits of UE salvage, too. Taking the time to work through this section will give you a fuller picture of your options.

As you can see, the third part of the worksheet has no space for quantifying values. Instead, the questions are subjective and open-ended. That's because establishing *benefit* is two parts art and one part science. How would you establish the benefit of UE salvage in these examples?

» *Jill used to be Mac's #1 salesperson, and she'd also been great at mentoring newer members of the sales team. Now her numbers and attitude were tumbling fast. But Mac knew that if he lost Jill, he'd lose much more than the sales revenue she brought in; he would also lose her ability to guide and develop new sales reps, which was invaluable to the entire team. What should Mac do?*

» *Zane worked harder than anyone else on his accounts team, yet seemed to accomplish little. His work was inconsistent, haphazard, and unpredictable, and he'd been like that since Lucille hired him four months ago. What is the benefit of keeping Zane?*

» *Nanci spent six months wooing Marc, the most experienced and innovative programmer in the region, from her competition. His salary was huge, and she quickly realized that his ego was just as big. His teammates were starting to avoid working with Marc. Should she stick by him, or cut bait in the interests of team morale?*

» *Bart was worried about Ari, a manager who reported to him. Ari's team loved him, but the milestones his department actually met were few and far between. Bart knew that a motivated team was worth a fortune in today's economy. How should he weigh the value of Ari's motivational leadership versus the goals that his team missed?*

◇◇

The Excuse-Maker

Benefits Can Be Hard to Measure

Think about raising a child to age 5. It's not difficult to quantify the cost of diapers, childcare, toys, and pre-school. But how can you quantify the value of his first smile, her first word, or his first step? If we didn't put a high value on those things, nobody would ever have kids! Similarly, it's hard to quantify the benefits of running a marathon, launching a new product, or even salvaging a UE—yet the cost of these undertakings is often all too painfully clear. In all these cases, if you just go by costs, you might miss a great opportunity.

On the other hand, if you just go by benefits, you might be prolonging your worst nightmare. That's why it's important to think specifically about the costs of replacing your UE. Is she a specialist? Does he have a skill that no one else on your team has? Is that skill hard to find in the general workplace? If your UE is a line employee whose skills are basic and easily replaced, the benefit of a UE salvage operation is relatively low. But if your UE is unique in some way, you have a lot more to lose by *not* getting him back on track. So use a little imagination to envision what your team would be like if your UE was able to turn himself around, and *then* compare those benefits to the cost.

Here is what Marcus wrote about the benefits that Jenny offered their organization:

Benefits of "UE Salvage"
Was your UE ever a fully productive employee? If so, what was his/her major contribution? Jenny used to be one of my star performers. At her previous level of performance, she could juggle old and new clients with ease and strong results. This brought in many referrals, helping everyone reach their goals.

Benefits of "UE Salvage"
What would this UE contribute to your team if he/she was functioning fully now? Maintain accuracy for current clients. Help retain long-term contracts with clients.
What incremental benefits from his/her participation might be captured over time? She might help win back some of our lost clients. She knows a lot of people at a lot of companies; perhaps she can informally help with business development?

Solution

After he'd finished **Part 3**, Marcus was in a very different frame of mind than he had expected. As he sat back and reviewed what he had learned by using **The "What's it Worth?" Worksheet**, he compared what he now understood to be the costs of *reacting* to Jenny's problem (at least $8,200 over the next six months, plus opportunity costs) with *attempting to solve* Jenny's problem (approximately $6,700). Those numbers were pretty close together, coming out in something of a wash. But the counter-intuitive surprise was that *giving up on Jenny* and replacing her might cost as much as $150,000. In addition, it would deprive his team of the potential benefits Jenny *could* bring if she changed—benefits that suddenly seemed a lot more enticing than they had before!

Result

Marcus was now ready to begin dealing with Jenny's problem head-on. **The "What's it Worth?" Worksheet** had helped him commit to a positive course of action, and he was ready to move on to **Step 2: Communicate**. Over the next few months, Marcus and Jenny worked through the other **5 Cs** together, and, gradually, Jenny stopped blaming others for her mistakes. This allowed Luca and her other colleagues to begin to trust Jenny again, which created a higher-performing team. And Marcus spent a lot less of his valuable time putting out fires.

Chapter 3 Summary

- *The first step in managing any unmanageable is to decide whether you will* **Commit or Quit**.
- *Filling out the entire* **"What's it Worth?" Worksheet** *will guarantee that you're looking objectively at all relevant factors, including the UE's impact on clients and coworkers, and the projected costs of replacing her.*
- *Whereas the costs of unmanageable behavior can generally be quantified, the benefits of conducting a UE salvage operation are less tangible. Use* **Part 3** *of* **The "What's it Worth?" Worksheet** *to consider your past experience with this UE, and your expectations for future performance.*
- *If you decide to attempt UE salvage, your next step is to* **Communicate** *the problem (see* **Chapter 4** *and* **Chapter 5***).*

Hot Tips	
If your UE says...	Try responding with...
"What's your problem?"	"Sub-standard performance is considered a problem in our organization. Where do you think your performance is above the mark? Where do you think it's below the mark?"

Hot Tips	
If your UE says...	Try responding with...
"I don't get what the big deal is."	"Let's unravel the problem into separate parts. That will help both of us understand exactly what the problem is."
"You blame me for everything. It's not fair!"	"How can we fairly evaluate the situation?"
"Everyone makes a mistake sometimes."	"You're right. And I want to help you succeed. To do that, we need to have open and honest communication."
"Would it be so terrible to cut me some slack?"	"My job is to keep the team moving forward. How would you evaluate everyone, including yourself, on the current team?"
"If other people were doing their jobs, I wouldn't be having trouble doing mine."	"What's the impact of someone not pulling their weight on a team?"
"I suppose you never did anything wrong, did you?!"	"I've made plenty of mistakes. And this conversation is about your current performance, so let's go back to that."

The Grumbler

In the previous chapter, you learned how managers can objectively decide whether to **Commit or Quit** when dealing with a UE. If you've decided to commit, the next step in a UE salvage operation is to **Communicate**. This is where you'll offer your view of the problem to your UE, and get her agreement that something is wrong. Until the two of you have reached an understanding about what needs to change, you'll be stuck in an endless loop of unmanageability.

Meet The Grumbler

Grumblers can be like broken faucets. At first, you're not bothered by a little drip. But as time goes on, and the complaints get louder, that little drip begins to feel like a steady downpour, and your team's morale starts to take a soaking. It gets even worse if other team members join in with The Grumbler, or react to his complaints by loudly voicing their own frustrations. If you don't put a stop to this situation, it can erode your team's productivity, stagnate future innovation, and cost your organization a great deal of money.

Case Study: The Endless Complaints of Aziz

Mary didn't mind managing someone old enough to be her father; in fact, she prided herself on her rapport with the Baby Boomer generation. No, it was Aziz's constant grumbling that bothered her. With the recent downsizing at their defense industry company, everyone was stretched too thin, and everyone complained occasionally; but Aziz's constant negativity was causing serious rifts on the team. Jose had stopped speaking to Aziz, Marcelle often argued with him, and Alexa tried to placate and moderate the tensions that had infected them all. These coping strategies were ineffective, and were causing a drop-off in productivity and focus.

Problem

Mary's first task—and your starting point, whenever you want to turn a UE into a productive employee—is to communicate with Aziz about the *problems* his unmanageability is creating.

That may sound easy but, counter-intuitively, many managers find that this is a tough thing to do. **Communicate** implies a *two-way* conversation, which means, by definition, that the two of you may disagree. Lots of managers dislike that prospect. They don't want their authority to be challenged, they don't want to argue with (or have to win over) a UE, and they'd much rather give a direct order (*"Stop complaining!"* or *"Do something with your attitude!"*) than hold an open-ended conversation. So why not just give direct orders? Why bother to discuss and mutually define a problem when you can just tell your UE what's wrong and how you expect him to go about fixing it?

There are two reasons: First, there's a chance that you don't know what the problem really is, and that whatever solution you plan to propose may not be the best one that's possible. And second, you want to get your UE's buy-in, and people are more likely to invest themselves in plans and ideas that they've helped shape.

Unless you have a very hierarchical company, most adults won't take "marching orders" (or at least not cheerfully) until they've personally bought into your plan. When you communicate with your UE up front, you will save hours of time and frustration further down the line. Not only will you benefit from his insight into what's really going wrong, but you'll also secure your UE's agreement to work with you toward change *from the very beginning*.

We're All Little Kids at Heart

When you think about it, UEs are a little bit like toddlers. If you've ever raised a toddler, you know that, without her cooperation, the simplest task becomes a battle of international proportions. Think back to when you were 6 or 8 or even 12 years old, and a parent or other adult ordered you (without discussion) to stop doing something you were doing. Whether or not you openly rebelled, didn't you feel indignant or resentful about having to change "for no good reason"? Do you remember what thoughts came to mind? Were they something like "*That's not fair!*" or "*There's nothing* wrong *with how I'm acting!*" or even "*You can't make me change!*"

Well, unfortunately, that's just what your UE will feel if you order him to change without getting his buy-in. You may be asking yourself how an adult can react so childishly, but psychologists have been wondering about that since Sigmund Freud invented psychology, philosophers have been wondering about it for 2,000 years longer, and nobody *really* knows the answer. Some people are remarkably mature, other people...not so much. But whether or not your UE generally acts like a 3-year-old, you can count on some very childish push-back if you approach him with a neatly packaged explanation of why he's wrong, and what he should do about it. Isn't it worth putting some effort into making sure that doesn't happen?

You Got a Problem With That?

They say that the spouse is always the last to know—and so is your unmanageable! In any unmanageable situation, *you* know there's a problem. Your *team* knows there's a problem. Half the people in your organization may well know that there's a problem. So who's the only person who *doesn't* know there's a problem? You guessed it: your UE, the person who's causing the problem!

That's why the first thing you need to communicate is a simple proposition: There is a problem. Obvious, right? Don't expect it to be easy, though, because your UE "likes" to do the problematic things he does. In fact, throughout this book, you'll see that unmanageable behaviors have a benefit for the UE. Some examples are *The Excuse Maker*, who successfully avoids responsibility by making excuses; *The AWOL*, who comes and goes as he likes because everyone has given up on him; or *The Gossip*, who gets all that nice attention from her peers for putting other people down. Your UE has been doing his thing for a while now, and so far it's gotten him what he wanted. So why would he want to change? (The answer is, he won't—unless you two can find a benefit of *manageability* that's more appealing to your UE than the benefit he's getting from being unmanageable.) So, don't be surprised if your UE resists even admitting there's a problem. If you persist, though (and we'll show you how to do that), you will eventually get through to him.

Once you've achieved your first success, the second thing you and your UE need to discuss is *exactly what the problem is*. There can be no forward motion until you agree on what's wrong, as Anne's client found out when she confronted her Grumbler. This didn't happen immediately, because even though Aziz was always quick to react negatively to every little suggestion or change (even when it turned out that change was for the better), Mary was used to ignoring him. But then Aziz's complaints began to get worse, and Mary told Anne at their weekly coaching session that she sometimes wanted to scream at him to shut up.

Solution

In the course of her coaching sessions with Anne, Mary became clear that what she wanted to focus on was not the problem that was currently in her face (Aziz's constant complaints), or even her reaction to it (anger), but the question of what lay *underneath* it. Although she was frustrated by Aziz's behavior, she wanted him to agree to the problem first, and then to see the impact of his behavior second. That would help her get to the *real* problem of decreased team morale. Here's what happened when Mary first tried to talk to Aziz about it:

Mary: *Aziz, I want to give you some feedback on a problem that I'm seeing.*

Aziz: *Okay. What problem?*

Mary: *In today's 15-minute meeting, you used negative words and a negative tone of voice five times. I'm hearing you complain and speak negatively more and more frequently these days.*

Aziz: *What is this? Big Brother? Were you watching me? Anyway, I'm just frustrated. If things were going better around here, I wouldn't complain so much.*

Mary: *Let's stay on track. I want to talk more about your words and tone of voice in today's meeting.*

Believe it or not, this was a good outcome to a **Step 2: Communicate** conversation. Tough feedback can throw *anyone* for a loop, and Aziz was actually more open and reasonable than many unmanageables would have been. If human relations were an exact science, every conversation would go the way you expect and hope; but, as things are, you can expect that your first effort at communicating with your UE—perhaps even your first few efforts—may fall short, as Mary's did. So take a lot of patience with you into UE conversations, along with the tips, tools, and insights throughout this book that will help you ultimately succeed.

Separate from the emotional dynamic, you can see that Aziz and Mary are at an impasse. Aziz thinks his complaining attitude is a reasonable *response* to problems on the job. Mary thinks his attitude *is* the problem on the job! No wonder he's trying to distract her with counter-accusations that, though they might have merit in some other context, function like "tit-for-tat" rejoinders, given the purpose of this conversation.

To return to the toddler analogy, remember when you were little and a playmate said, "*You're being mean*"? Did you say, "*Ah, yes. You're clearly upset. I can see your point of view, even though I disagree with you about my responsibility for what's happening*"? Of course you didn't! You probably said something like, *"I'm not being mean. You're being mean!"* And then your friend probably said, *"No, you're the meanie. Meanie, meanie!"* This is basically what Aziz said to Mary, and it's to Mary's credit that, even though she was stung by his words (the "Big Brother" comment made her furious), she wisely ignored Aziz's provocations and put the conversation back on track.

When a UE provokes you, *don't engage!* Don't respond to his accusations. As the manager, it's your responsibility to rise above verbal temptation, and ignore any counter-hits or digressions. Keep the conversation on task, and firmly focused on the problem at hand. Rather than engage in he-said she-said, look for objective confirmation that what you're telling your UE matters.

What You Do Is (Often) What You Get

Hard as it may be, when you're beset by negativity, the best way to encourage an upbeat attitude at work is to demonstrate what it looks like to have one. That doesn't mean "whistling while you work," like the Seven Dwarfs in Snow White. It means showing your team that challenges can be met with calm determination instead of constant complaining.

You can also set a more subtle tone—say, one that encourages teamwork and productivity—through actions, as well as words. One of Anne's clients wanted to set the tone of openness, because that was one of his company's values. To do that in a non-verbal way, he created an office layout for himself that was open-spaced, and had no walls. This meant that anyone could approach him with feedback at any time. He also let his direct reports set the agenda for weekly team meetings. This reinforced their feeling of empowerment and created team-wide buy-in for whatever was decided at the meetings.

SOPs and UE Behavior

Most organizations have SOPs, or Standard Operating Procedures, that are generally written in a document, handbook, or manual.

SOPs outline the organization's methodology for completing tasks, so that every employee knows exactly what steps to take when completing the task at hand. This allows the organization to create standard practices and to deliver uniform products or services.

Sometimes the SOP manual will also spell out the conduct that's expected of an organization's employees. If your organization has an employee manual or other written compendium of Standard Operating Procedures, check *before your first conversation with your UE* to see if it covers the behavior you hope to change. If your company does not have SOPs in place, look for best practices online or through colleagues and associations, to get a sense of what your peers and the experts are saying about the problem you face. (You may also decide to ask your organization's senior team to form a task force to start crafting organizational SOPs. They're a useful tool that will benefit you and your colleagues in personnel-related situations.)

Most SOPs can be expected to cover theft, absenteeism, and other behaviors that are universally recognized as unprofessional; but what about "soft" behaviors and skills? Does your firm's employee manual discuss rudeness? Gossip? Inappropriate humor? If you're lucky enough that this is the case, you can have a straightforward conversation like this one, held by a Sales Call Center client that Anne advised:

Bert (the manager): *Kendra, I just saw you hang up on a caller in the Sales Call Center. What was going on?*

Kendra: *That caller was an idiot. I kept telling her that item #7732 is sold out, but she wouldn't believe me. I knew there was no use trying to convince her, so I hung up.*

Bert: *What is our policy on handling client complaints or caller challenges?*

Kendra: *The policy is to escalate up to a manager if I can't handle the call.*

Bert: *Did you do that?*

Kendra: *No.*

Bert: *So did you violate one of our company policies?*

Kendra: (pause) *Yeah, I guess I did.*

Because the Sales Center's SOPs were on record, Bert and Kendra quickly reached agreement about what the problem was. Kendra couldn't say, "I don't understand what's wrong," because hanging up on a caller was clearly against the SOPs, and she knew that Bert knew it.

Try and Try Again

In this case, Mary had hit a wall with her first try at convincing Aziz that his constant naysaying was a problem for her team. She'd also turned up nothing in her company's SOPs that would help her show Aziz that his behavior was unacceptable. But Mary wasn't ready to give up on Aziz. After speaking with Anne in her weekly session about how hard it is for anyone to change their behavior, Mary decided to try again, this time putting Aziz's naysaying into context. Here's how the conversation went:

Mary: *Aziz, we talked about this before, last week. But I still heard you complain three times in yesterday's meeting.*

Aziz: *I told you, I'm frustrated!*

Mary: *That's right; you said that. What's the team likely to think, when they hear constant complaining?*

Aziz: *I haven't thought about it.*

Mary: *Well, let me ask you this: Who else is working harder since the lay-offs?*

Aziz: *Everybody's working much more than we did last year.*

Mary: *Do you hear other people grumbling?*

Aziz: *Maybe once in a while, but not...*

Mary: (after a pause) *Not what?*

Aziz: *I guess they don't complain as much as I do.*

Small Concession, Big Breakthrough

Doesn't sound like much, does it? But for Aziz, admitting that he naysays, grumbles, and complains more than other people was a breakthrough—and the first sign of possible success that Mary had been looking for.

Now Mary was ready to push a little harder on the *impact* of Aziz's behavior, which is the second part of communicating the problem. If a UE has no awareness of the impact he is having on others, there is no reason for him to even consider changing his behavior—and the reverse is also true. Here is how Mary got Aziz to focus on his impact:

Mary: *So how do you think other people feel, if you complain more than they do?*

Aziz: *How do I know what they're feeling?!*

Mary: *Well, what might you feel if you were in their shoes?*

Aziz: (after thinking for a minute) *Ticked off, I guess.*

Mary: *Hmmm. Anything else?*

Aziz: *Maybe they're thinking, "I don't want to work with him!"*

Mary: *Do you think that's possible?*

Aziz: *If they're tired of listening to me....*

Mary: *Aziz, I don't want to see that happen. You're a valued member of this team.*

Aziz: *I don't want that to happen, either.* (sheepishly) *This job isn't that bad.*

Mary: *Hey, I'm really glad to hear that. And I know an exercise that could help us make sure that you don't lose the team's respect.*

Open the Toolkit

By now, you've noticed that getting UE buy-in is a series of little steps. First, your UE must agree that there's a problem (and what it is). Then you need to agree on the impact of the problem (because many UEs will cheerfully admit that they're doing something "wrong," but continue to claim that it's no big deal.) Just like Mary, you have to take it one step at a time, and build toward a point where your UE admits there's a problem, agrees with you about what the problem is, and has begun to consider the problem's impact.

When these three things have been accomplished, you and your UE are ready to cooperate on finding a solution—and you're ready to dip into your toolkit. Turning to a tool at this point in the process lets you and your UE use an objective approach and problem-solve together. It isn't you telling him what to do; it's the two of you collaborating to find a solution that will benefit everyone. Of course, that doesn't mean you'll instantly agree, or that changing unmanageable behavior is easy! It means that your UE has begun to buy into the goal of fixing the problem he created. You can then introduce the tool you've chosen, as Mary did with Aziz in their next conversation:

Mary: *Aziz, I'd like to* **reset our working relationship**. *Let's get clear on what's important to me, what's important to you, and how we can bridge the difference.*

The Trade-Off Tool

In Chapter 3, you learned about **The "What's it Worth?" Worksheet.** This is a tool that you work with *alone,* to help you decide how much value a particular employee represents to your company. Once you've decided to commit, though, the rest of the tools in this book are for two. You and your UE will use them together, to create buy-in and mutual solutions.

As you can see from the chart on the following page (and the copy you'll find in **Appendix B**), **The Trade-Off Tool** involves several simple steps. First you list the areas of behavioral conflict (or, in a new relationship, possible conflict) between yourself and your UE. We've listed some common conflict areas in the sample here, but if the conflicts in your organization are not on our list, write those down instead. Then one of you writes down each of your preferences for how to behave in that disputed area.

The Trade-Off Tool	
Behaviors (sample list)	**Fill Out for Each Behavior That Applies**
Interactions Attitude Language Deadlines Punctuality Success	My Preference: Your Preference: The Gap: The Solution:

Now here comes the emotional challenge. Put aside for a minute any feelings you might secretly (or not so secretly) have that your way is the right way and that what the other person wants is totally unreasonable. Then, engage in an open-minded discussion of the gap between your two perspectives and the possible ways you might bridge this gap. Here's how Mary and Aziz handled that conversation:

Mary: *Aziz, we've agreed that complaining is making problems for you and me—and maybe for others on the team. Let's fill out The Trade-Off Tool and see how we can bridge the gaps between how we'd each prefer to handle this issue.*

Mary had printed up a copy of **The Trade-Off Tool,** and now she filled in the behaviors she wanted to address with Aziz.

Mary: *I can tell you that my preference would be, nobody on my team ever complains.*

Aziz: *That sounds totally unrealistic! My preference would be to be able to say what I feel, and have people know I'm just blowing off steam.*

Mary filled in both their answers, and noted that the gap was wide. She said:

Mary: *We're pretty far apart on this. But there should be something in between all and nothing-at-all that we can work with.*

The Trade-Off Tool: Mary and Aziz	
Behaviors	Fill Out for Each Behavior That Applies
Naysaying Grumbling Complaining Negativity	Mary's Preference: No complaining!
	Aziz's Preference: Unlimited complaining!
	The Gap: All or nothing-at-all.
	The Solution:

"Ain't No River Wide Enough..."

Don't assume that the widest gaps are the hardest ones to bridge. We've all been in situations in which someone else dug in his heels about what seemed to us to be a very small difference (whether to grill or broil a steak or whether to set the thermostat to 68 or 69 degrees—that kind of thing). And even though it's counterintuitive, the reverse is also true: Sometimes the widest rivers are the easiest ones to cross. So don't get discouraged when the gap between your preferences and those of the person you're negotiating with seem large. Remember that a big gap can give both parties more room to maneuver and, again, counter-intuitively, a greater chance at success.

Perhaps in response to her open attitude, Aziz then made a startling admission:

Aziz: *You know, when I make negative comments, I'm trying to give direct and clear feedback. It makes me angry when people don't want to hear it.*

Mary: *I want to hear what you're thinking!*

Aziz: *Really? You're willing to hear the good* and *the bad?*

Mary: *Yes, I am—but it makes me angry when you badmouth ideas and shoot them down. I'd rather hear your comments in a more positive form.*

As she heard herself saying these words, Mary realized what the trade-off might be:

Mary: *Aziz, complaining under your breath is not positive or productive. Coming to me directly and telling me your thoughts is. Could you do that if I promised to listen, and not blow off your comments as grumbling?*

Aziz: *Yes, I think I could make that work.*

Mary: *I'll commit to doing that, if you commit to keeping your tone and attitude positive when delivering the message.*

Aziz: *I'll try my best. Please point it out if you hear me grumbling again. It may take me a while to get used to being positive.*

Mary: *Deal.*

Mary filled in the final line of **The Trade-Off Tool** to reflect the agreement they'd just reached:

The Trade-Off Tool: Mary and Aziz	
Behaviors	Fill Our for Each Behavior That Applies
Naysaying Grumbling Complaining Negativity	Mary's Preference: No complaining!
	Aziz's Preference: Unlimited complaining!
	The Gap: All or nothing-at-all.
	The Solution: Aziz will give his feedback directly to Mary, and try to do it in a positive way. Mary will listen to his critique, and not dismiss it as complaining.

This is where all your creativity as a manager comes into play. And the managerial skill that you'll develop through this exercise—the ability to encourage and foster teamwork—is exactly the one you most need in today's globalized, Web 2.0 world. That's because most organizations now ask their employees to overcome differences and collaborate intensively. When you can guide your team through that process, as Mary did with her UE, Aziz, you'll strengthen their camaraderie, and their ability to succeed.

Once you and your UE have reached a compromise—no matter how tentative or unproven it is—write down exactly what actions the two of you have agreed on. This will be your road map to accountability. If either of you forgets what was agreed upon, you can refer to the written document. If either of you backtracks, the document can be used to get back on track by saying something as simple as *"We agreed that I'll listen respectfully to your feedback in exchange for you not being negative with the team,"* or *"We agreed to use e-mail as our mode of communication. I've received three texts from you this week. Can we please stick to our agreement?"*

And though you can never truly "restart" a relationship (the things that happened between you in the past can never go away), try to stay true to the spirit of the phrase *relationship reset*. This phrase implies that both people are willing to move forward from today. Be sure to evaluate your UE by how he behaves from this point on. Don't hold past mistakes against him.

Sometimes It's a Generational Thing

Differing habits, beliefs, and expectations, some arising from our backgrounds, can lead to conflicts or misunderstandings at work. If you believe that differences in gender, nationality, religion, class, generational identity, and so forth may be wrongly contributing to the appearance of unmanageability, speak with your organization's diversity leader for information and advice.

Generational styles and cultures are a prime example of diversity conflicts at work. Right now, there are three major generations in the workplace—Baby Boomers, Generation X, and Generation Y (also known as Millennials)—and each has its own culture, priorities, and style. (**Appendix A** presents detailed information about generational preferences, language, and working styles.) Often, what appear to be unmanageable situations may turn out to be misunderstandings between generations, such as these:

- *John, a 50-year-old Baby Boomer, likes to send long, detailed e-mails that explain what he needs so that he "won't be misunderstood." Andrea, his 33-year-old Gen X direct report, would much prefer to receive concise bulleted information, or a text. John is fast concluding that Andrea doesn't respect his thoughtful analyses (and therefore him). He also thinks that Andrea doesn't care about her job because she "blows through" his e-mails without paying close attention to them.*
- *Marie, a 25-year-old Gen Y employee, and her 45-year-old Gen X boss Ferdinand, are both big football fans. Unfortunately, their shared passion does nothing to bring them closer together because Marie chats about last night's game on Facebook (where she can share video clips, hyperlinks, and photos), and Ferdinand relives it in the cafeteria (communicating with hand gestures and reenacted play-by-plays). Ferdinand thinks that Marie is not a team player (why isn't she sharing last night's victory?), and Marie refrains from making technical suggestions because she believes that Ferdinand is too "old school" to understand or appreciate them.*

The moral of these stories is this: As you walk through our **5 Cs Framework** with your UE, be aware of generational and other differences that may be creating or worsening an unmanageable situation. Also, remember that each generation has its own "personality" and culture. **The Trade-Off Tool** is particularly useful for negotiating conflicts that stem from generational differences.

Three Tools in One

The Trade-Off Tool is great for resolving unmanageable behaviors, but it also has many other uses. Rather than waiting for trouble to develop, you can use it at the *beginning* of a relationship to establish agreed-upon ways for people to communicate, handle deadlines, define success, and much, much more. You can also use **The Trade-Off Tool**'s *principles* in a casual conversation, rather than a more formal sit-down, by asking questions such as *"I prefer texting; how do you like to be contacted?"*

If a minor conflict is already underway, **The Trade-Off Tool** can be a tremendous time-saver. Not only does it contribute to fast resolutions, but it also allows you to solve early-stage disagreements before small frustrations and misunderstandings have grown into unmanageable situations. In this case, you may want to sit down with both parties for a matter-of-fact and cordial conversation.

Finally, if a conflict has become large or troublesome, **The Trade-Off Tool** becomes a life-saver, because it allows you to reset the relationship. In this case, it makes sense to use **The Trade-Off Tool** as part of a more formal process. We recommend that you:

1. *Make a list of the behavioral areas that you believe need to be better defined.*
2. *Consult with your company's policy manual or HR department to learn what rules already exist (as Mary did with Aziz's naysaying).*
3. *Call a meeting of all interested parties—ideally at a turning point such as the beginning of a new project, so that everyone can make a fresh start.*
4. *Bring out The Trade-Off Tool and explore ways to fix the problem, or reach compromises that will head a problem off.*

One caveat: As with all the other tools in this book, **The Trade-Off Tool** exists to help you explore and understand *what your UE wants*. You can also use the tool to get a better understanding of *what you want*—but don't do that step with your UE. Just as a lawyer doesn't ask a question if she doesn't already know the answer, you don't want to hold a team "negotiation" until you know the outcome you're trying to create. You can always change your mind and decide that a better outcome is possible, but never sit down to deal with a UE unless you know your own bottom line, and are willing to fight for it.

The Grumbler

Result

In the months that followed, Mary and Aziz both stayed vigilant about holding each other to their negotiated trade-off. There were definitely some bumps in the road, but in time—thanks to Mary's persistence and **The Trade-Off Tool**—Aziz made the journey back from being an unmanageable employee to being a fully engaged and productive one who only grumbled now and then. No matter what behavior *your* UE exhibits, **The Trade-Off Tool** will help you structure that all-important first conversation, negotiate for new behaviors, and keep your UE firmly on track.

Chapter 4 Summary

- *Once you* **Commit** *to a UE salvage operation, your next step is to* **Communicate** *the problem, and gain agreement about what's gone wrong.*
- *Many UEs do not understand the impact of their behavior. Getting them to acknowledge their impact on others is an important step toward creating change.*
- *If your organization's SOPs or employee manual discusses the type of behavior at issue, share this information with your UE.*
- *Use* **The Trade-Off Tool** *to set boundaries that the UE will agree to live within. (You can also use the tool in new relationships and when small conflicts have begun to percolate.)*
- *Continue to monitor your UE to make sure he is honoring your negotiations.*

Hot Tips	
If your UE says...	Try responding with...
"I'm the only one who does any real work around here."	"What's your biggest contribution to the team?"

Hot Tips	
If your UE says...	Try responding with...
"If other people would step up to the plate, I wouldn't be so frustrated."	"How could the team become more effective?"
"I'm just blowing off steam."	"What's the impact of that on the team?"
"I'm just being me."	"You have talents and skills. How can you bring them even more to the forefront?"
"This is how people from my background talk."	"What's the value of that type of talk to our team?"
"What's wrong with a little healthy conflict?"	"Nothing, as long as it's respectful. What does respectful conflict look like to you?"
"Why are you so upset about what I said?"	"Language can be easily misinterpreted. Tell me three ways that your statement might be perceived by others."

5

The Egomaniac

In the previous chapter, you learned how to use **The Trade-Off Tool** in situations in which conflicting preferences need to be negotiated. But people often disagree about what's gone wrong between them, let alone about how to resolve their conflict. That's because we all like to feel that we're in the right (and are behaving impeccably), and UEs are no exception. Many unmanageables are in denial about the situation they've created. They don't want to face the negative impact their behavior is having on others—or even on their own careers—and will say things such as, *"You're entitled to your opinion, and I'm entitled to mine. Mine is that you're making a big deal over nothing."*

Words like these are a clear signal that it's time to explore the difference between your UE's stated intentions and how his actions are perceived by others. In this chapter, you'll learn how to use **The Perception Gap Tool** for a UE reality check, how to help your UE see the problems he's creating, and how to move forward with the process of UE salvage.

Meet The Egomaniac

In today's fast-paced, hyper-competitive global environment, the pairing of big ego and big success is a familiar one (think Donald Trump or Dennis Rodman). But the same ego that drives some people to succeed can also drive their colleagues to distraction. And the situation gets worse when an Egomaniac's manager is conflicted about holding this UE to the same standards of behavior that others must meet. Letting an Egomaniac run wild can lead to jealousy, misplaced competition, and an "us vs. him" mentality on the part of other team members—and it can leave a manager confused about just how to hold her team together while their morale is spiraling downward.

A healthy ego can be a good thing, if it motivates people to act assertively and to persist in the face of discouragement. But taken to the extreme of egomania, it can cause the demise of an entire team. If everyone is getting along and working well together, and if productivity has not being negatively affected, there may be no need for concern. But keep an eye on the situation to make sure that things don't change, as they did in the following case study.

Case Study: Ruby's $2 Million Ego

As VP of advancement at a major state university, Jada supervised a small, successful team that included her star fundraiser, Ruby. Although others resented "Queen Ruby's" ego, Jada was inclined to look the other way when Ruby dodged routine tasks and paperwork, in part because Ruby had recently secured a $2 million donation for the university. But Jada's moment of truth came when she asked Ruby to mentor a new hire, and Ruby told her, "That would be a waste of my time. I'm focused on the big bucks, not the little people." Clearly, Ruby had drawn a line in the sand between herself and the rest of the team. It was time for Jada to take action—fast.

Problem

Because Jada was confident that her Egomaniac was worth salvaging (this is often the case with strong performers), she was ready to move directly into **Step 2** of **The 5 Cs: Communicate**. But Jada wasn't entirely clear about *what* she wanted to communicate to Ruby. Did she want to make the point that other team members disliked working with her? (It seemed possible that Ruby wouldn't care.) Did she want to stress that this animosity toward Ruby was hurting their team? (Again, it seemed likely that Ruby would be disinterested in this news.) Was there some way to appeal to Ruby's bottom line, which was clearly her own self-interest, and define the problem in those terms?

After considerable thought, Jada decided to stop worrying about what she wanted to communicate, and focus instead on what she could learn from Ruby's view of the situation. Was Ruby aware of how others reacted to her? Did it bother her? Was there a **perception gap** between what Ruby thought she was doing and how other people saw her motives? Jada actually hoped that there was, because that would give her a clear way forward, and something concrete to discuss with her UE.

The Perception Gap

All of us have felt the shock of finding out that something we did or said was heard or received very differently from how we meant it. That's what happened in the following situation:

> *After a night meeting that ran late, Jessie gave her friend Lawrence a ride home. As they were driving through the dark, Lawrence became concerned that Jessie's dashboard lights were set too low. At the next stop sign, he reached over and, without stopping to consult Jessie, raised the light level, just as he often did for his wife.*

Jessie was very offended by this. She took Lawrence's well-meaning but clumsy action as a direct insult to her and her driving. The difference between what Lawrence *intended* (to create safety) and how Jessie *perceived his intent* (to criticize and interfere) is called a perception gap.

Close relationships and chronic stress are two of the factors that can increase the width of a perception gap. Although many people are willing to give strangers the benefit of the doubt, that can (ironically!) be more difficult to do when you care about someone, or when you're in a stressful situation. You may have noticed this dynamic at home. Many people find that it's more difficult to stay cool, calm, and collected with their families than it is with relative strangers. It seems counter-intuitive (because don't our loved ones deserve our best?), but sometimes we're on our best behavior with people we don't know as well—and that can include being more tolerant of their annoying actions. As your team begins to gel, and your team members get closer (and more like a family), you may notice that tempers flare more easily, particularly when the team is under heavy stress. This common dynamic is easy to spot once you know to look for it, and, along with the **perception gap**, can help explain the intolerance and impatience you sometimes see among people who work closely together.

If you believe that your UE's issue is being compounded by a perception gap, **The Perception Gap Tool**, shown here, will help you explore and understand the problem in a conversation with your UE. In the earlier example of Lawrence and Jessie, their perception gap was 100 percent (they were as far apart as they could get): Lawrence intended his behavior to be helpful, but Jessie perceived it as insulting. Here's what that looks like in **The Perception Gap Tool:**

The Perception Gap Tool (Use this chart to record intentions, perceptions, and the distance between them.)		
Lawrence's Intention: help Jessie drive more safely by giving her more dashboard light		
100		100
90		90
80		80
70		70
60		60

50		50
40		40
30		30
20		20
10		10
Jessie's Perception of Lawrence's Intention: insult and interfere with her driving		

Whether it occurs in a friendship or a work relationship, a giant perception gap such as this one spells trouble if it's not confronted and narrowed. But imagine how different this gap might have looked if Lawrence had simply *mentioned* his concern to Jessie, rather than taking unilateral action. In that case, the gap would almost certainly have been much smaller—more like a 20-percent distance, as the next chart shows. (You can illustrate a smaller distance between intentions and perceptions by crossing out lines, or folding the paper **The Perception Gap Tool** is printed on.)

The Perception Gap Tool (Use this chart to record intentions, perceptions, and the distance between them.)		
Lawrence's Intention: help Jessie drive more safely by pointing out the low dashboard light		
20		20
10		10
Jessie's Perception of Lawrence's Intention: make a well-meaning, if unneeded, suggestion		

89

Preparing to Succeed

The Perception Gap Tool isn't just a way to think about and measure private rifts. It can also help a manager explore the tensions on his team, and help a UE—in this case, an Egomaniac—better understand how his intentions are being perceived by others. Before you have this conversation, though, you'll need to prepare.

If you were going to give an important business presentation, you might try to think it through, write down at least part of it, and practice out loud beforehand. This is also the best way to approach a difficult conversation. Don't assume that the right words will come to you when you need them. If you think through what you want to say in advance, you'll have more confidence and feel better able to respond appropriately and effectively—no matter how your UE reacts! As you prepare your thoughts, ask yourself these questions:

- *Am I saying what I really mean (or hinting around the subject)?*
- *Am I describing what I've observed (and not just venting my own feelings)?*
- *Would I be inclined to listen if someone said these things to me, in this way?*

Now it's time for you to practice. No matter how thoroughly you think things through, and no matter how good your thinking looks on paper, you won't know for sure if you're really prepared until you hear your own points delivered out loud. The best way to practice for a tough conversation is to role-play it with a friend, mentor, or colleague. Does your practice partner understand your point? Are you getting the reaction you expected? Based on how the run-through went, do you want to change how you approach your UE in the upcoming conversation? Don't worry if the answer is yes; that's what this prepare-and-practice stage is all about.

In addition to getting your message right, practice the nonverbal side of your communication. You could have the best argument in the world, but if you deliver it mechanically, or with fear, or aggressively, your UE will tune you out. So while you're practicing your message, also ask yourself:

» *Is my tone reasonable and firm?*
» *Am I speaking slowly and clearly, so that my UE can hear the words I'm saying?*
» *Am I leaving silences so that she can react or respond?*

Again, this may seem like a lot of trouble to go through for a short conversation. But remind yourself what's at stake here. If some advance preparation helps you to salvage a top performer *and* your team, isn't it worth the effort?

Solution

After thinking carefully about the situation, Jada decided to use **The Perception Gap Tool** to communicate the feedback she was hearing from the team about Ruby. She still wasn't sure how much Ruby would care, but thought this approach was worth a try. So Jada asked Ruby to stop by her office first thing the next morning for a talk. That night, Jada wrote out some ideas for how to communicate with Ruby in a way that was clear, flexible, and non-judgmental. She also ran through the conversation with a friend. When Ruby arrived at work the next day, Jada was ready.

Jada began by telling Ruby how much her work was appreciated. *"The donations that you bring in have made great things possible at this university. I know you could make much more money someplace else, so your loyalty is particularly valued."* Ruby nodded pleasantly; after all, what Jada was saying was the simple truth!

Jada then said, *"We both know that the donors love you. How do you think you're viewed by your colleagues?"* Ruby thought that over before she answered, *"I think they're jealous of me. They need my numbers to make them look good, but they know I don't need them for anything."* This was the opening Jada had hoped for. She said, *"Are you sure that you don't need them? Don't they do your paperwork?"* This is how their conversation continued:

Ruby: *Sure they do, but let's be real. Anyone can push paper around. Nobody else can do what I do. I don't have anything against them; they're just irrelevant in my eyes.*

Jada: *I actually see it differently. To me, your team supports your success. If I required you to handle your own paperwork, you wouldn't be able to make as many donor asks.*

Ruby: *You wouldn't do that! That would be crazy.*

Jada: *I agree. But to me, that indicates that you do need the team to be successful.*

Ruby: *You could look at it that way. But I'm the one whose work is directly helping the university.*

At this point, Jada handed Ruby a blank **Perception Gap Tool.** She said, *"I'd like us to use this tool to quantify how far apart our perceptions are. You see yourself as a kind of lone ranger, riding out every day for the good of the school. I see you as somebody who can't or won't be a good team player, and who doesn't appreciate the help you get."* Ignoring the slight look of hurt in Ruby's eyes, Jada added, *"With that in mind, could you please complete this chart?"*

Ruby started to fill in the tool. When she finished, it looked like this:

The Perception Gap Tool (Use this chart to record intentions, perceptions, and the distance between them.)
Intention: I'm all about the university. I work hard, and I'm damned good at my job. Instead of getting appreciation, I'm getting complaints because I don't like paperwork.

The Perception Gap Tool (Use this chart to record intentions, perceptions, and the distance between them.)		
100		100
90		90
80		80
70		70
60		60
50		50
40		40
30		30
20		20
10		10
Perception: Jada thinks that I'm just out for myself, my own glory, I'm not a good team player, and I don't appreciate what other people do to help me.		

Jada reviewed Ruby's notes, and said, *"Given what you've written here, how far apart are we?"* And Ruby answered, *"About as far apart as you can get. No wonder it's feeling tense around here."* Because Jada hadn't been sure that Ruby was even aware of the tension people felt around her, she took that comment as a good sign.

Jada: *You're right. Things have been tense around here. Now tell me your intentions for the university. It sounds like they're very high.*

Ruby: *You bet they are. This place gave my mom a scholarship 30 years ago, when nobody was supporting women in science. After graduating, she got a job with a biotech firm and was able to give her kids a good life. If it wasn't for this university, I don't know what would have happened to us.*

Jada: *That's a very powerful story. I'll bet you tell it to all your donors—and I'll bet none of your teammates know it! Speaking of which, can you tell me your intentions toward your teammates?*

Ruby: *I think my intentions toward them are good. I want everybody to succeed.*

Jada: *I'm pretty sure that's not how they see it. Several of them have mentioned to me that they don't want to work with you—just like you've said you don't want to work with them. Do you think that's okay for the team?*

Ruby thought hard before answering, which, again, Jada thought was very positive.

Ruby: *Truthfully, in the short run, I don't care if they don't want to work with me. I bring in enough donations by myself. But I'm not going to be here forever—and if I'm your only star performer, fundraising could all fall apart when I leave.*

When Jada heard that, she had to work hard to keep from smiling. It wasn't the most gracious assessment, but this was the first time Ruby had admitted that having a strong team actually mattered to her. It had taken a great deal of work on Jada's part to make Ruby aware that alienating her teammates was a problem for the university, even if Ruby herself didn't care.

Plant a Seed

As you can see, one of the tough things about communicating with UEs is that you've thought about the problem in advance, but they're confronting it for the first time. Your thinking is comprehensive and has developed over time, but they may be struggling to think past what you're saying right now. And whether or not they say it out loud, your UE may be thinking things like *"How dare you criticize the way I do my job!"* or *"I didn't know people resented me!"* or *"I can't believe you're giving me a hard time, considering my results!"* or *"I don't really care what people think!"*

You'll have to summon a lot of patience to ignore these distracting reactions and help your UE grasp her new reality. So even though you may be eager to get the situation sorted out *now*, be prepared to slow down your process, move at a pace your UE can assimilate, and accept small breakthroughs as they come.

And though it would be easy to just wrap up your meeting as soon as your UE has admitted there's a problem, take the time to consolidate your gains by first asking a **coaching question** to give your UE a little push forward. (You'll learn more about how to ask effective coaching questions in **Chapter 10**.) The coaching question Jada asked was:

Jada: *It sounds like your colleagues don't perceive your real intentions toward the university. What would help them see you more clearly?*

Ruby: *Maybe I should tell them about my mother.*

Jada: *If you do that, let me know how it goes.*

As you'll learn in **Chapter 10**, this was a good coaching question because it's *open-ended* (Ruby can't shut down the conversation with a yes-or-no reply), *short* (Ruby is less likely to tune out), and *advice-free* (Jada never states her opinion). Questions like this can encourage a UE to think about her situation in a whole new way, and begin to point her in the direction of change.

Why The Perception Gap Tool Works

The Perception Gap Tool exploits our natural desire to be liked and respected by those around us. You can see the power of this desire if you think about its impact on our personal lives. We want to look as successful as our neighbors (so we try to keep up with the Joneses). We want our actions to be interpreted favorably (and when they're not, we try to save face). Our concern with making a good impression is so strong that we even have a mental health diagnosis for people who don't feel those pressures (sociopath). This desire to meet community norms is at play in every part of our lives, include the part we spend at work.

Is Life Like Junior High or Middle School?

Have you ever walked into a room full of strangers or people who outrank you in some way, and suddenly felt as though you'd been catapulted back through time to junior high school? Junior high, or middle school, is the time in most people's lives when issues of being liked and accepted are at their sharpest and most painful. Many adults are confident extroverts who love wading into a crowd of new people. But other people in the same situation will feel niggling insecurities about being exposed that are all too reminiscent of the feelings they had when stripping down for gym class. This dynamic can work to your advantage when you're dealing with your UE. Like most people, your UE wants to be liked and admired by her peers, whether she admits that openly or not. If you can appeal to that basic desire, your UE may change her behavior accordingly.

All of this is good news for the manager of a UE like Ruby, because, no matter how intractable a UE may seem to be, chances are good that she cares *at some level* about the impression she makes on others. In Jada's case, **The Perception Gap Tool** worked because, in spite of her Egomaniac attitude, Ruby did care (at least a little!) about what other people thought of her.

Another factor in Jada's success was the directness and honesty of her feedback to Ruby. Rather than stand aside and judge, she involved Ruby in a collaborative process of defining and solving the problem together. That's both the goal of this step and the reason why it's so powerful.

Results

Although Jada realized that Ruby's personality would never change, she was happy that, once Ruby's eyes had been opened to how her teammates regarded her, she began to treat them more like people and less like pieces on her personal chessboard. Gradually, the tensions lessened, and Jada was able to bring everyone together for some brainstorming about how to smash their fundraising goal. This gave Ruby a way to share her insights and experience without overdoing the ego factor, and the whole team's morale began to lift. (In **Chapter 7** and **Chapter 8**, you'll learn about how official and unofficial roles on a team can impact manageability.)

Although it's difficult to contend with an Egomaniac's outsized sense of entitlement, it's worth the effort if that means salvaging a productive employee. You can lessen the tensions your Egomaniac creates by appealing to this UE's self-interest, and by using tools such as **The Perception Gap Tool** to demonstrate that ego-driven actions are impacting her bottom line.

Chapter 5 Summary

- *Most people care how others view them—and this applies to most UEs as well.*
- **The Perception Gap Tool** *helps you illustrate the difference between a person's intentions and the way those intentions are perceived by others.*
- *Often, revealing that gap will help a UE buy into changing his behavior.*
- *Once the problem has been acknowledged, you can begin to solve it by using all of* **The 5 Cs** *and tools as resources.*

Hot Tips	
If your UE says...	Try responding with...
"I'm worth two of your other employees."	"In addition to your actual donor dollars, what other value do you add to the team?"
"Other people are just jealous of me."	"What's the impact of jealousy on the team?"
"If you don't like it, why don't you just fire me?"	"How would it help the department if I fired you?"
"You don't want to get into a power trip with me!"	"You're right! What's our common ground?"
"I work best when I have room to maneuver."	"How can our team maneuver together?"
"I'm the best, and that means never having to say you're sorry."	"How does the organization benefit from that attitude?"
"I've made you look very good, haven't I!"	"This isn't about you or me. This is about the organization and our team. Let's stay focused on that."

The Loose Cannon

It's important for *every* employee to understand his or her organization's goals, and his or her own role in achieving those goals. Without the clear direction that knowing goals and roles provides, *any* employee can become lost, frustrated, and, ultimately, unmanageable. But nowhere is this clarity more important than for the UE.

Meet The Loose Cannon

Loose cannon is a term that's typically associated with someone on the lower end of the performance scale. However, a high-performing Loose Cannon can be much more challenging to manage, and an abrupt transformation from *favorite child* to *trouble child* is not unusual among top performers. These superstars tend to be extremely dedicated, confident, and bright. They often don't take direction easily, and people may hesitate to rein them in for fear of cramping their productive style. Yet, when high performers become disenchanted or think that their input isn't valued, the situation can quickly turn unruly, because a high-performing Loose Cannon can pack a tremendous amount of firepower.

Case Study: From Superstar to Super UE

Andrew, the superstar fund manager of a small investment firm, was becoming a giant pain in the organization's butt. His manager, Cheryl, was tired of arguing with him about the company's direction. He just wouldn't get with the program, and had lately started going over her head to complain directly to her boss, Sam. Now everyone was ducking Andrew's e-mails, he was calling in sick (when he wasn't), and Cheryl was thinking that she might have to let her star performer go.

Problem

Andrew's current investment firm had lured him away from a previous employer with the promise that he could develop a fund to support small, sustainable, international businesses, with a strong focus on Africa. A passionate advocate for green growth, Andrew was thrilled to be building a portfolio that let U.S. investors make money and support deserving small businesses.

For a year, he traveled non-stop to prepare for the launch of this new fund. He did feasibility studies, made recommendations to the board, courted A-list celebrity donors, and, most of all, worked hard to select the most viable and exciting businesses to support. *Everything* was in place for success.

But three months before the fund was due to launch, Andrew's boss, Cheryl, called him into her office to say that they wouldn't be moving forward in Africa. Her boss, Sam, the investment firm's managing director, had decided to shift the fund's target area to another region where the political and financial climate was more favorable for their goals.

Andrew was devastated. In a year of traveling through Africa, he had cultivated business owners who were counting on him to deliver funds. It didn't make sense to him that the firm was changing direction, let alone key goals, now—and he said so, loudly, vehemently, and often. When Cheryl stated that the decision was out of her hands, Andrew simply went over her head and started harassing the firm's managing director, lawyers, and Board chairman.

It was clear to Cheryl that she was going to have to intervene. Not only did she want to salvage this unmanageable, but she also wanted to re-establish her managerial authority and her connection with Andrew. Because it's often difficult to bridge interpersonal gaps via e-mail, Cheryl decided that her interactions with Andrew should occur in a real-time, *old school* format: face to face.

Why Meet Face to Face?

Before the Internet and cell phones made everyone immediately available to everyone else, face-to-face meetings were the default way of doing business. In someone's office, at the job site, and often over a meal, colleagues and collaborators sat down for one-on-one interactions that were *personal* in every sense of the word.

Today, face-to-face meetings have gotten a bad rap because they so often waste everyone's time. Making people travel a long distance to transact some business that could have been done on Skype or by e-mail is a good way to infuriate your team. So is making them sit in a stuffy conference room for an endless discussion of something they don't care about. There are meetings in which nothing valid is said and meetings in which nothing noticeable gets done. There are meetings that seem to have no other purpose than stroking the ego of the person who called them. All of these (repeated) experiences have turned people off to face-to-face interactions.

Yet there are times when only a face-to-face will do. Those times include (a) when the stakes are high, (b) when the potential for misunderstanding or offense is great, (c) when tensions are already off the chart, and (d) when difficult news is being delivered. Three of these considerations were operative for Cheryl: She needed to meet with Andrew in person because the stakes were high, tensions were mounting, and the potential for misunderstanding was great. And although her content could have been delivered by phone, fax, or e-mail, it's much harder to build trust that way. Cheryl needed to sit in a room with Andrew and observe the small glances, the true tone of his voice, and the details of posture that can't come through in a video conference, let alone an instant message.

When Cheryl contacted Andrew to arrange a meeting, she half-expected that he would say it wasn't necessary. That's because older generations tend to opt more quickly for face-to-face interactions than younger ones. (See **Appendix A** for more information on how each generation prefers to interact.) But Andrew, who knew that his situation was serious, immediately agreed to meet with Cheryl. Now all she had to do was figure out what she was going to say to him!

Applying The 5 Cs

The question of how to bring a superstar back from the brink of unmanageability is a tough one; and, in general, your most productive approach is prevention, not cure. For example, superstars are used to being part of the decision-making process. They want and expect to be kept in the loop about high-level goals or changes in policy. So for your sake, as well as your UE's, be sure to keep him informed—at the earliest possible moment—if changes are coming that will affect his work. This is where Cheryl went wrong with Andrew: As natural as it is to want to put off giving bad news to your best performer, letting him hear about it after the fact or from somebody else is a good way to put him on the road to unmanageability.

Unfortunately, in Andrew's case, the time for an early intervention had long since passed. That's why Cheryl thought carefully about what could be done at this stage of his UE slide. Finally, she called Joyce—who'd been Cheryl's mentor at a previous job and who had a good touch with interpersonal problems—and asked for help in working out a plan of approach. They met for a late dinner that night, and came up with this analysis:

Step 1: Commit or Quit

This one was a non-starter for Cheryl. There was no question of losing Andrew's talent, particularly because of a problem that (although she felt he was handling it "badly") he hadn't created in the first place.

Step 2: Communicate

Cheryl dreaded this step of the process, but Joyce gently reminded her that Cheryl's fear of confronting Andrew had only made the situation worse. With that in mind, Cheryl told Joyce her answers to **The 10 Communication Questions,** a tool added in Chapter 2.

The 10 Communications Questions	
1. What problem is my UE presenting?	Becoming a Loose Cannon; won't accept a change in the firm's direction
2. Do I have any sense of the root cause of the problem?	He probably feels misled and disappointed after a long effort
3. What's the impact of the problem on my UE's performance?	Very disruptive
4. What's the impact of the problem on my team?	Can't pursue new goal without him on board; also threatening my status
5. What actions have I taken so far?	None
6. How has my UE responded to those actions?	N/A
7. When will I hold a conversation with my UE?	Never? (Just kidding! Sort of...)
8. What are the main points I want to get across?	I was wrong to not tell you sooner the way things were going, but how you're acting now won't change anything except to damage your career
9. What are the questions I might ask my UE?	What would it take for you to buy in to the MD's new priorities?
10. How will I know if the talk is a success?	Andrew will meet me at least halfway in looking at new goal and direction

After completing this exercise, Cheryl felt more confident that she could hold a productive conversation with Andrew. For the first time, she thought that it might be possible to resolve their problem.

A Frank Conversation

The next day, after she and Andrew settled into the leather visitors' chairs in her office, Cheryl took a calming breath and launched into the conversation.

Cheryl: *Andrew, I want to talk to you about the new direction of the fund. But first, I need to apologize for a couple things that I handled badly.*

I should have told you the first time I realized our MD was reconsidering Africa. I know how much that meant to you, and, frankly, I was a little scared to bring it up. I didn't give you any warning, and that just made it worse in the end.

The second thing I wish I'd done differently was to fight harder when Sam changed the plan. I don't think I'd have won, but I regret not going to the mat for you. I'm very sorry about those things.

But now that the decision has been made, you and I both have to live with it. And I want to know—are you willing to talk with me about how we can move forward from here?

As Cheryl had hoped, Andrew agreed to at least talk about their situation. Importantly, she had set the stage for cooperation by starting with an effective and appropriate apology. Cheryl calmly explained her mistakes and repeated that she was sorry about them. She didn't dramatize or excuse, and she didn't dwell on her feelings. She also didn't press Andrew to react, but gave him the courtesy of space and time to consider what she'd said. Her tone and her words showed respect for them both.

This kind of apology takes prior thought (so that you understand what you're apologizing for) and a lot of self-confidence. Many people think that they're apologizing when they're really either blaming (*"I'm sorry that you made me lose my temper"*), condescending (*"I'm sorry you feel bad"*), or deflecting responsibility for their actions (*"I'm sorry for whatever you think I did"*). It takes courage and clarity of mind to apologize for *only what you truly regret* ("*I wish I had told you as soon as I knew that things were going to change, and I apologize for not doing so.*") in a sincere and responsible way. Cheryl's ability to meet this challenge played a large role in preparing Andrew to move with her into **Step 3** of their process: **Clarify Goals and Roles**.

What Goals Mean to an Organization

Cheryl's mentor Joyce had suggested that the problem with Andrew could productively be thought of as one around misaligned **goals**. Agreed-upon goals are the bedrock of an organization's success, because they create a consensual, far-reaching vision of what an organization is trying to achieve. Sometimes goals can be articulated in a mission statement; this, by definition, means that the goals will be general and broadly stated. Other times, when goals are more specific or immediate, they can be expressed in clearer details.

But whether they're specific or broad, general or detailed, clear goals keep everyone on course because your entire team knows where they're headed. If your goal is to go to Honolulu, you're not going to spend time researching travel information for London or Kabul. You're going to research Honolulu. You may choose different modes of transportation (boat or plane?). You may take a different path to get there (east to west? north to south?). But you always know exactly where you're going. And if you get off track and suddenly find yourself stranded in Fiji, you'll know how to correct your course, because you'll know that you have to get to Honolulu—somehow, some way. Honolulu is your goal. That's where you're headed.

Cheryl and Joyce felt that, in Andrew's case, a new organizational goal had been defined, documented, and assigned to him by upper management. The problem was that nobody had discussed the change with *Andrew*, who learned about it after the fact, by memo. Because of his passion for the old goal and his status as a top contributor, this was the worst possible strategy for creating buy-in. (It created unmanageability instead.)

Using the Goals Diagnostic Chart

In order for organizational goals to be implemented effectively, they must be well defined, clearly communicated, accepted by the employee, and fully documented. (Organizational roles, which have parallel requirements, are discussed in **Chapter 7** and **Chapter 8**.) If even one of these steps isn't followed, it's easy for confusion and chaos to ensue.

Goals Diagnostic Chart

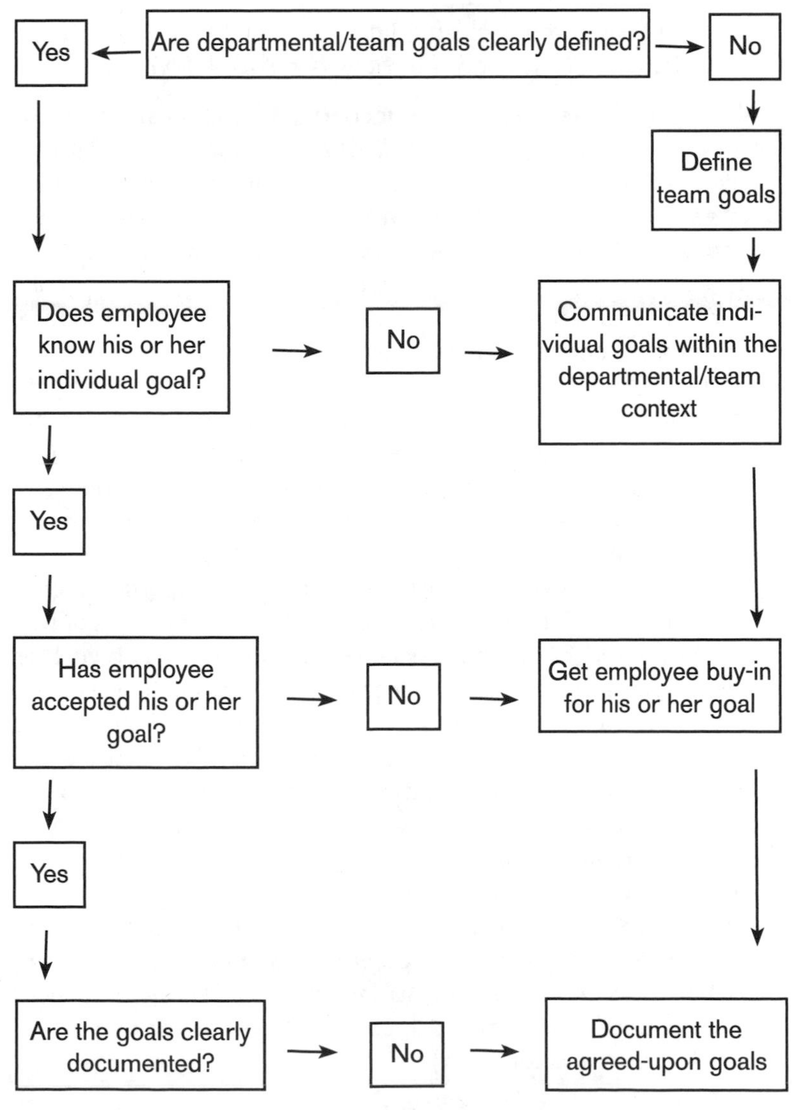

◇◇

The Loose Cannon

There are four basic steps in **The Goals Diagnostic Chart:**

1. *Clearly define the departmental/team goals.*
2. *Communicate individual goals, within the departmental/team context.*
3. *Get each employee's buy-in.*
4. *Document the goals that have been agreed on.*

Many managers start with the second of these four steps, saying, *"Your goal is to track the repeat client ratio in our hotel."* This certainly meets the requirement of communicating an individual goal, but because you skipped Step #1, the employee doesn't have a sense of the big picture—of *why* her particular goal is important. Completing Step #1 and defining the big-picture goal creates a very different level of understanding, and, usually a very different response. So instead of communicating a goal such as, *"Track our repeat client ratio,"* try saying, *"Our company wants to reward returning clients through a new incentive program. To do this, we need to know what percentage of our guests are return customers. Our team is in charge of calculating that ratio, and I'd like you to be in charge of that, since you have the most experience in this field. Is this opportunity of interest to you?"*

Once your UE understands *why* she's being given a particular goal, she'll be much more likely to commit to it. And getting that kind of employee buy-in for your team's overarching and smaller goals is vital for everyone's success. You will know that you're getting employee buy-in when your conversation about the new goal leads to excitement and enthusiasm instead of resentment and frustration (which indicate low levels of buy-in). And if you do get resentment about this goal, take a step back and try asking open-ended questions, such as *"On a scale of 1 to 10, with 10 being the highest, how enthusiastic are you about this goal?"* When you get the answer, you can then follow up with *"What would notch that score up by 2 points?"* Or, you might ask, *"You seem frustrated. What's frustrating to you about this goal?"* (As you'll see in **Step 4** of **The 5 Cs: Coach,** open-ended questions like these can help you and your team members talk about and resolve many types of underlying issues and concerns.)

Solution

Cheryl now felt confident that talking to Andrew about goals would be useful. Here's how she did it:

Cheryl: *Andrew, how would you define the firm's* **goals** *with regard to your fund of sustainable small businesses?*

Andrew: *That's easy. The goal is to encourage green business growth in Africa, while creating a vehicle for U.S. investors.*

Cheryl: *You know, with the exception of the words "in Africa," we agree completely. Do you think that a commitment to Africa was part of the original reason for this fund?*

Andrew: *I don't know; I wasn't working here when the fund idea was first created. But Africa was definitely key to the plan at the time that I was hired.*

Cheryl: *My sense is that setting up a high-quality fund to attract new investors was the primary goal, and that helping a particular region was always secondary, and subject to change*

Andrew: *I thought this was all about Africa. I might not have come onboard if I'd known that you didn't feel the same way.*

Cheryl and Andrew thought about that for a minute. They were both struck by how one small difference in the framing of a goal had ultimately created a big rift on their team. Again, a seemingly small mistake in how you set the course for your team or an employee can make a big difference in the outcome.

Goal-Setting 101

People need goals, and not just in a philosophical sense. Goals play a central, anchoring role in job satisfaction. Most people want to know what they are supposed to be doing; what their purpose is at work. It is disconcerting to be misaligned with your colleague or team, and not knowing your team's *true* goal makes it virtually impossible to succeed.

That's why employees whose goals are unclear, unspecific, or uncertain are at greater risk for unmanageability than employees whose goals are clearly specified, communicated, and documented. Even if your employee doesn't *agree* with the goals you've communicated to him, he is more likely to handle that disagreement responsibly when everyone involved has clarity about what his goals *are*.

As you probably know (and may have learned the hard way), not every goal is a *practical* or *effective* goal. To make sure that your goals will work, test them against these three criteria:

- *Are your goals "outcome-centered"?*
- *Do they answer the question "So what?"*
- *Are they SMART?*

By creating goals that meet these criteria, you can help your employees understand *not just what's expected*, but why it matters. This, in turn, will help to reduce the unmanageable frustrations that people feel when their days are filled with endless "to do" lists, instead of being filled with meaningful work.

Outcome-Centered vs. Task-Oriented Goals

Goals (no matter what their content) tend to fall into two categories: the ones that stand alone (*task-oriented*) and the ones that serve a larger purpose (*outcome-centered*). Implicit in an outcome-centered goal is the idea that *your action will have an impact on others*, whereas task-oriented goals are just *tasks to be executed.*

Often, the difference between the two comes down to the context that's provided. For instance, take these task-oriented goals:

- *Write two chapters of the new policy manual by June.*
- *Sign up 10 new clients for our product this quarter.*
- *Hire three new people by December.*

Although each of these *tasks* can be executed on its own terms, think about the difference it would make if they were re-framed as *outcome-centered goals*:

- *Get input on the policy manual from 50 percent of new employees, so that (new hires can enter our organizational culture effectively). If appropriate, draft two chapters.*

- *Inspire 10 clients to try our new product and (enhance their life-work balance) (by September). Speak with the entire team about what messages clients respond to best.*
- *By December, try to hire three new people who fit well into our team, (allowing our department to grow with little attrition).*

See the difference? Outcome-centered goals are not about activity for its own sake, but about getting things done *because getting them done* supports your organization's *mission*. Not surpisingly, it's much easier for employees to buy in to goals that have a rationale, a desirable impact, and a clear connection to your organization's mission, because these goals answer the question *why*, which increases employee motivation. It also helps that outcome-centered goals are often more specific, easier to follow, and more inclusive than mere tasks.

On the other hand, task-oriented goals create resentment and alienation. We all feel like we're drowning in tasks—"G*et back to accounting.*" "*Finish that memo.*" "*Put in for John's vacation.*" "*Buy milk on the way home*"—and being given more of them can make us feel like cogs in a machine instead of people with a purpose. Task-oriented goals don't build toward anything. They just keep coming. And coming. And coming.

So as you think about clarifying goals, remember that the goals themselves have an impact. When employees complain about having too much work, the *type of goals* they're being asked to meet often turn out to be part of the reason. Remember: Task-oriented goals drain energy, whereas outcome-centered goals generally create buy-in. Try to create outcome-centered goals that remind your UE of her value to your team—and see if that reduces her frustration with work, and your frustration with her!

So What?

The second criterion for effective goals is that they answer the question, "*So what?*" When you're looking at the "*So what?*" factor, you're looking at your goal from a higher level, and reminding yourself of why that goal is important. "*So what?*" is another way of asking

"What's the impact of this goal?" "How does this goal support the big picture?" and *"What will someone else feel, know, and/or do differently when I've met this goal?"*

Creating goals with the *"So what?"* factor goes *beyond* creating outcome-centered goals. That's because, although an outcome-centered goal explains *what* the goal aims to achieve, asking *"So what?"* adds the question of *why* that outcome is worth achieving. In the three previous examples, *"So what?"* versions of the goals might be:

» *The policy manual will be started with input from 50 percent of the new employees, allowing me to help new hires enter our organizational culture effectively. The HR team will reduce the time they use to answer questions when this manual is in place.*

» *Ten clients will be inspired to try our new product by September, which will enhance their life-work balance and allow our team to win the incentive trip to the Bahamas.*

» *By December, I will hire three new people who fit well into our team, allowing our department to grow with little attrition. This will allow Mary to reduce her workload and Jose to take paternity leave without impacting the rest of the team.*

SMART Goals

In addition to being (a) outcome-centered, and (b) answering the question, *"So what?"* effective goals are (c) SMART. The SMART acronym—sometimes attributed to management consultant and professor George T. Doran—has been around for more than 30 years, and has proved useful to countless managers. There are many interpretations of what SMART means. We find the most useful one to be: **Specific**, **Measurable**, **Agreed-upon**, **Relevant/realistic**, and **Time-based**. To make sure that your goals are SMART, make them:

» **Specific.** *For example, look at the goal "We will improve our data input." Although this goal seems* *specific, it leaves a lot to the employee's imagination. What part of the "data system" are you going to improve? The input? Analysis? Quality? Quantity? Be more specific, so your team knows what to focus on.*

- **Measurable**. *Your team wants to know what targets you're aiming for, so be sure to make their goals measurable. "We will increase data input by 22 percent over the next nine months" is a measurable goal, whereas, "We will improve our data input" is not. With the first goal, everyone knows what target to shoot for: 22 percent over nine months. With the second one, everyone can define "improve" in their own way, which can often lead to confusion, uncertainty, and recriminations.*
- **Agreed-upon**. *Many managers will set a goal without thinking of its impact on their team. Improving data input by 22 percent might be an impressive achievement, one that will surely win the team some awards. But is it truly possible? And what will it cost the team to achieve it? Will they be able to do it by increasing productivity by 10 percent, which is feasible? Or will they need a 50-percent increase, which may result in burnout and attrition? Did the team give any input to the new goal? Creating a new goal without feedback from the team could cause problems. So take the time to discuss potential goals with your team before setting them. Gather their ideas, get their input, and get you on board before making a final decision that everyone might regret later.*
- **Relevant**. *Adults learn best when something is relevant to their daily life, so make sure that your team's goal is relevant to the organization's mission, the department's goal, and/or the goals of individuals on your team. If employees are given an irrelevant goal, they may put it aside or ignore it.*

The Loose Cannon

- *Goals should also be* **Realistic***. If the team says yes to increasing productivity, they will likely have to say no to something else (like new projects) while they are focused on this goal. Be sure that everyone understands the implications and impacts of the goal they're agreeing to. And when you set a stretch goal, be sure it's one that is achievable with a slight stretch outside your team's comfort zone. Great leaps are daunting, and can backfire if people aren't really ready for them; smaller stretches are much more achievable, relevant, and realistic.*
- **Time-based***. Time-based means that your goal is anchored in time. To do this realistically, set a SMART deadline for the goal, (say, a 22 percent increase in productivity, and then work backwards to what must happen for this to occur. Map out clear benchmarks on the calendar, so that everyone can see them and work toward them. Check in on a weekly basis to ensure that the benchmarks are achieved each week, and that your team is on track to reach its goal. Remember that, without benchmarks, your "goal" is actually a "fantasy"!*

Keeping Your Team Up to Date

Once you've created team goals that (a) are outcome-centered, (b) answer the "*So what?*" question, and (c) are SMART, what else can you do to help your employees—including any UEs—commit to and achieve their goals?

First, ensure that everyone is clear about their short-term goals, and your goals for the team. To do this, hold regular (brief!) team meetings where everyone concisely explains their goals for the coming day or week. (The simplest way to ensure brevity is to hold the meeting with everyone standing up.) Then, review the *team's* goals for the same day and week, to ensure that everyone is on the same page. If anyone seems to be misaligned or unsure about their goals for this period, ask that person to stay behind, and clarify the situation immediately.

To ensure clarity about *long-term goals*, review your team's and department's strategic goals quarterly and annually. At these meetings, to create greater buy-in, give people the time they need to offer input and develop ideas. And before any of these meetings adjourn, confirm and record every team member's goals so that everyone knows your expectations for the quarter. Then follow up on a regular basis to ensure that those goals are met on time.

Finally, as your team's *"communicator-in-chief,"* remember that no one meeting, e-mail, or memo is enough to guarantee that people will remember, let alone act on, what they've heard. In general, people need to hear something six times, in different ways, before they absorb it. So don't just send an e-mail about your team's goals. Send e-mails, hold meetings, post signs, do a video, create a postcard, talk about them. Obviously we all have different ways that we prefer to communicate, and you may be in the habit of reaching your team through just one channel (leaving phone messages, or e-mailing them). But that's even *more* of a reason to surprise your employees—and get their attention—by changing channels now and then. If you're used to giving instructions in person, leave a voice message. If you usually leave voice mails, send a text. You could even create a communications *campaign* to make sure that a particular message is heard, using face-to-face this week, phone next week, e-mail the week after that, and so forth.

Bottom line, do whatever it takes to be sure that every employee knows their goals, and the goals for your team and organization—along with how reaching their individual goals will contribute to *everybody's* success. And even though we'd all love to be heard and understood the *first* time we say something, don't assume that your campaign isn't working until you've made at least six tries. (If you're not getting through to people at *that* point, use the coaching questions discussed in **Chapter 10** to find out why.)

Solution

Following her conversation with Andrew, Cheryl did some thinking about the way she'd presented his new goal.

It seemed clear with 20/20 hindsight that she'd given him a *task-centered* goal (*"Focus the fund on a different region"*) rather than explaining in detail why her MD, Sam, had changed the focus from Africa, or what the modified goal would achieve for their firm.

No wonder he'd bristled at the new goal! Not only was he being asked to compromise the relationships with donors and small businesses that he'd spent more than a year cultivating, he'd also been asked to do it in a *non-outcome-centered way* that didn't affirm his contributions or the firm's mission.

Cheryl realized that the solution to Andrew's unmanageability issue was for her to (a) speak with her boss, Sam, about whether any compromise could be reached, while also (b) reframing Andrew's new goal so that he could make sense of the sacrifices he'd been asked to make.

Result

Cheryl started with a meeting with Sam. She realized she had never given Sam's new direction much thought; she had just accepted it and moved on. Now, she wanted to understand the bigger picture—the reasons for Sam's change.

Sam showed Cheryl some of the international reports he'd consulted in making his choice. Many of these discussed the potential volatility in the region they had targeted in terms that, Cheryl had to admit, gave pause. The reports were from highly trusted sources, and did raise a serious issue about whether the program that they'd planned was a safe use of donor money. That being the case, Cheryl conceded that it did seem to make sense to change course for now.

The question was: Where would they invest next? Sam had some ideas of his own, but he was willing to listen to Andrew's suggestions—particularly after Cheryl explained why she thought that being left out of the loop had triggered Andrew's unmanageability.

This gave Cheryl the hook she needed for her next conversation with Andrew. When they met again, Cheryl and Andrew discussed the international reports together. Although Andrew still wasn't pleased with Sam's decision, he grudgingly admitted that Sam had grounds, and perhaps this wasn't the best time to invest in the region they'd originally chosen.

Cheryl asked Andrew to recommend a new part of the world for the program to target. Andrew spent several weeks immersed in research before presenting his ideas to her and Sam. During this time, it was striking to Cheryl that Andrew's unmanageableness subsided. Being asked for input and invited to discuss goals had made all the difference in his attitude. And once the new region was selected, Andrew threw himself into the job of building contacts in that area. He was now invested in the firm's new goal, and he quickly became a star performer again.

If your UE's performance is going south, take a step back and clarify goals—with the UE, and with your entire team. This activity will help everyone understand what they're responsible for, and more importantly, *why*. It will also quickly reveal any areas of confusion, and show you where your own communications with the team need to be strengthened. Clarifying people's goals will eliminate task-based resentment, and will show your UE—and everyone else—what they must do to stay on track.

Chapter 6 Summary

- *Goals should ideally further your organization's mission, and vision of what it's trying to achieve.*
- *Misaligned goals cause can unmanageability, and turn superstars into super-UEs.*
- *Outcome-centered goals empower people. Task-oriented goals, like endless to-do lists, can frustrate and demotivate employees.*
- *Keep your goals* **SMART** *(Specific, Measurable, Agreed-upon, Realistic/relevant, and Time-based).*
- **The Goals Diagnostic Chart** *will help you determine where the conflict over goals between you and your UE originated. The steps to take are:*
  - *Clearly define the departmental/team goals.*
  - *Communicate individual goals, within the departmental/team context.*
  - *Get each employee's buy-in.*
  - *Document the goals that have been agreed on.*

◇◇

The Loose Cannon

» *If you make a mistake, apologize! Employees will trust and engage with you more if you're honest and transparent with them.*

Hot Tips	
If your UE says...	Try responding with...
"Why are you hassling me? I do a good job!"	"Tell me how you define/ describe your job."
"I want to do what I signed on to do."	"What's your understanding of what you signed up for?"
"You don't know what you're doing."	"How would *you* handle this situation?"
"I should have been part of that decision."	"If you had been, what would your ideas have been?"
"It's a stupid decision."	"What's a smarter decision?"
"I can prove that you're wrong."	"Tell me more about your ideas."
"I'm the expert in this area. You're just the boss."	"How can your expertise help us solve this problem?"

7

The Joker

In the previous chapter you learned how misaligned goals can cause unmanageable situations and unruly employees. Your UE's understanding of his role on the team also plays a vital part in any UE salvage operation. The more clearly a role is defined, assigned, accepted, and documented, the easier it will be to transform a difficult situation into a successful one. In this chapter, we'll see how unclear roles contributed to the misbehavior of another UE: The Joker.

Meet The Joker

Some managers find it hard to believe that a Joker can become a UE. After all, who doesn't want to work in a fun, jovial work environment? Yet too much of anything can become a liability. If one of your employees is constantly making wisecracks and joking with the clients, the office environment can teeter on the brink of unprofessionalism, causing customer service complaints and lost clients. In addition, just like in the story of Peter and the Wolf (about a little boy who cries *"Wolf!"* so many times that no one believes him when a real wolf shows up), it's hard for a Joker's colleagues to know when to take him seriously and when to dismiss his antics. This can erode The Joker's credibility, and hurt his career path and prospects.

Case Study: Send in the Clowns

Ian is a young pediatrician who recently joined a prestigious, mid-sized group practice. His older colleagues appreciate his superb clinical skills, but Ian's biggest fans are his "pint-sized patients," whom he tickles, teases, and entertains with imitations of Jim Carrey characters. Unfortunately, his patients' parents are less than enthralled with Ian's humor, because he can't seem to settle down long enough to answer their serious medical questions.

Problem

Mrs. Latrelle was not the first person to complain to Ian's supervisor, Blaine, about Ian's attitude. But whereas other parents had made tentative comments (*"Ian is just like a big kid"*), Mrs. Latrelle was openly critical, saying, *"My daughter's asthma isn't funny, and I think it's unprofessional for him to joke about it. If he can't speak to me appropriately, I'm going to have to find another doctor."* With that comment, Blaine knew that Ian's behavior could no longer be laughed off.

Because managers are human too, it's easy to err on the side of caution—sometimes even putting your head in the sand and avoiding difficult situations until something forces you to confront them. That's okay, but be aware that the longer you wait before taking action, the more time there is for things to go wrong and for the problem to compound itself. It's like being in a fender-bender that quickly expands to a 10-car pile-up. So remember that you're the manager, and sooner or later (hopefully sooner), you're going to have to face your problem head-on.

Take Time to Think

Because he'd been in a bit of denial, Blaine needed some time to reflect on what to do about Ian. So late that night, after dinner with his family, he went up to his home office with a glass of wine, his iPad, and some notes about **The 5 Cs**. (For Blaine, who is an introvert, this quiet note-taking session worked in the same way that talking things through with a mentor or friend works for people who are extroverted.)

When a Talker and a Thinker Communicate

In the world of personality theory, an introvert is someone who likes to reflect on issues. An **extrovert**, on the other hand, prefers to talk about the issues with others. Introverts can find it stressful to have their thought process interrupted, and extroverts can stress when they're expected to come up with answers by themselves. These differences can create tension between you and your unmanageable if she would rather confront an issue and talk out what's wrong **right now**, while you would rather write down your thoughts and reflect on what to say before conversing (or vice versa). Fortunately, as with most communication problems, understanding the source of tension can be half the battle. Think about the differing communication styles in play, and decide if you want to use **The Trade-Off Tool** (see **Chapter 3**), or can just talk things through.

As he worked methodically through the first few steps of **The 5 Cs**, Blaine could see that some would be easier to implement than others. For instance, Blaine considered Ian an excellent doctor, and had no interest in losing him. So his **Step 1: Commit or Quit** decision was already made. But **Step 2: Communicate** struck Blaine as potentially much trickier, for three reasons:

- *Ian was passionate about his patients, but much less concerned about their parents' needs.*
- *Blaine didn't want to "pull rank" on Ian. Though he had the authority to correct, or even sanction, Blaine didn't want to create resentment in a valued junior colleague.*

» *Finally, though Blaine was no psychologist, it seemed to him that things would go best if he could somehow motivate Ian to change—and do that in their initial conversation.*

With that in mind, he pulled up a copy of **The 10 Communications Questions**, and typed the answers into his iPad:

The 10 Communications Questions	
1. What problem is my UE presenting?	Playing The Joker at work
2. Do I have any sense of the root cause of the problem?	Focused on amusing the kids, and taking it way too far
3. What's the impact on my UE's performance?	None, he's a great doc
4. What's the impact on my team?	Potentially serious, if parents start leaving the practice
5. What actions have I taken so far?	Basically none; half-heartedly brought it up once
6. How has my UE responded to those actions?	N/A
7. When will I hold a conversation with my UE?	As soon as I can figure out what to say
8. What are the main points I want to get across?	Without the parents, none of us would have a job

9. What are the questions I might ask my UE?	How can you interact with parents to get the best outcomes for their kids?
10. How will I know if the talk is a success?	For this conversation: he acknowledges the problem and we talk about solutions. For the long term: Ian acts more professionally; there are no more parent complaints.

Finding a "Theory of the Crime"

As soon as he reached question #9, Blaine knew he'd discovered a clue. Maybe Ian didn't understand that part of his role was to partner with his patients' parents to get the best outcomes for their children. And perhaps he didn't yet realize that parents were also *customers,* because they (along with their insurance companies) were the ones who paid the bills.

In pursuing this train of thought, Blaine was acting like an "unmanageability detective." If you like watching crime shows or reading mystery novels, you know how hard the police often work to come up with a theory of the crime. In a sense, you're doing the same thing when you explore different possible answers to the question *"Why is my UE acting like this?"*

One of the main places where you'll try to get that puzzle solved is on your **Step 2: Communicate** conversation with the "perp" (oops, we mean the UE!). Sometimes you will truly have no idea what's motivating your unmanageable's behavior—and that's fine, because, ultimately, he's the only one who knows the truth, the whole truth, and nothing but the truth. But if you have a theory about what's going on, don't hesitate to bring it forward *in a non-blaming way.* Just be prepared (as a cop or detective has to be) to adjust your theory when new evidence comes in. If you ask your UE *"Do you resent that I promoted Sally instead of you?"* and he says *"No,"* open your mind to the possibility that something entirely different may be going on. And don't worry if it takes you more than 46 minutes to figure out what that something is. The only place where complex mysteries routinely get solved in less than an hour is on TV cop or detective shows.

In this case, the more Blaine thought about his "theory of the crime," the more he felt that Ian's behavior might be the result of confusion about one aspect of his role. If that was the case, the problem was serious, but easy to address using **Step 3: Clarify Goals and Roles**.

What's the Role of Roles?

In Chapter 6, you saw that clear organizational goals are vitally important to achieving success—and the same thing is true of roles.

What's the difference between these two things? Whereas a *goal* provides direction that will get a group of people where they want to go, a *role* is always personal and specific. Roles are *the actions assigned to every person within a group or organization.* To return to the example in Chapter 6, if your team is going to Honolulu, each person on the team will have a role that helps the team achieve its goal. Are you the pilot? Co-pilot? Flight attendant? Baggage handler? Every person can ask *"What's my role?"* because everyone will have a role to play, no matter how big or small it is.

Clarifying roles is vitally important to achieving the team's goal. If one of your employees thinks his role is *"pilot"* when it's actually ensuring that the jet has fuel, your team will soon run out of fuel, and no one will get to Honolulu. And if two people each think *they're* the jet fueler, they'll be duplicating each others' efforts—jostling each other as they both fuel the plane, while some other important role goes unfilled.

How do you handle this, as a manager? Although many people may potentially be able to fill a particular role, your job is to find the *best* person for it. Who has the best combined aptitude and attitude? Where are each person's talents best utilized? Finding the right role for each employee is an art and a science, because no one fits into the glass slipper perfectly. It's up to you to work with what you have, first filling each role with the person you choose, then helping that person expand to best fill the role.

Roles Diagnostic Chart

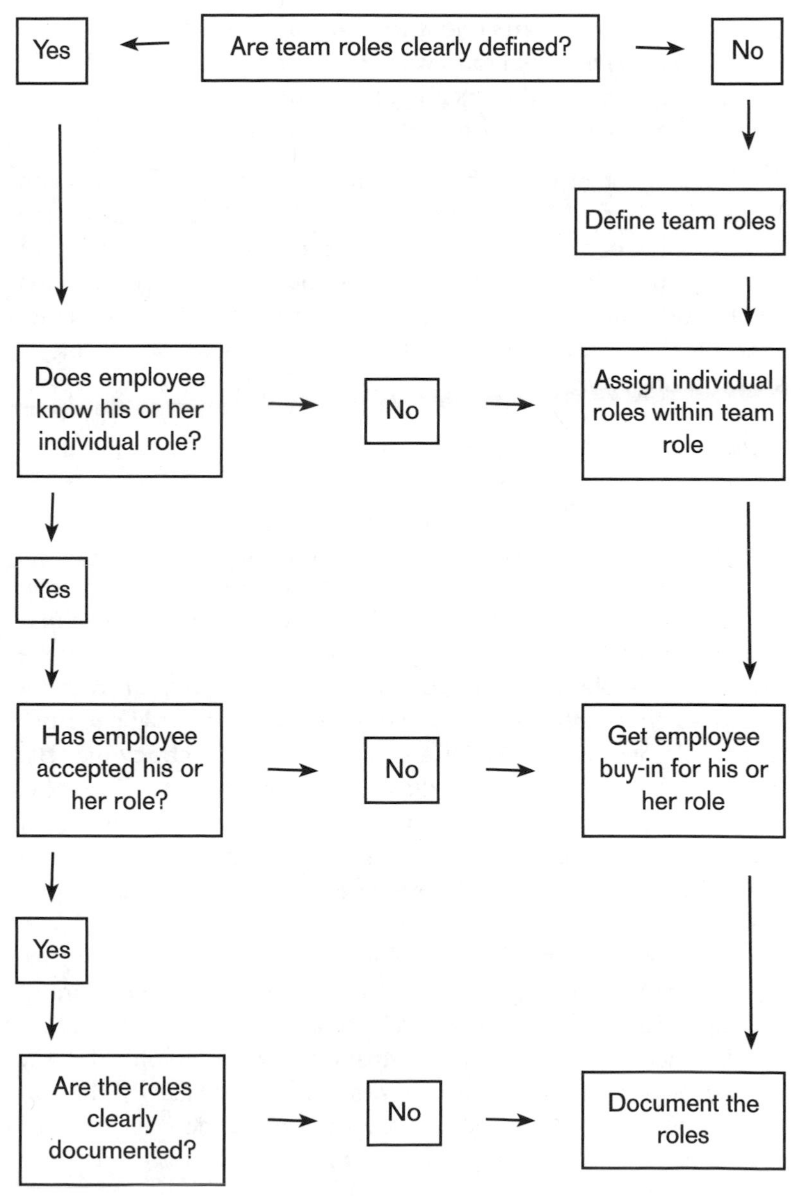

The Joker

As you'll notice, this chart parallels the **Goals Diagnostic Chart** in **Chapter 6**, which also includes four basic steps:

1. *Define the team's role within the organization.*
2. *Assign individual roles within the team's role.*
3. *Get each employee's buy-in for his or her role.*
4. *Document the roles that you've assigned.*

When it comes to the first step, many managers ask, *"How can a team have a role?"* To understand that, think of your organization as a complex ecosystem, with each department doing its part for the larger organization. One team's role may be to ensure that the organization's documents all comply with the letter of the law (that's generally the Legal Department). Another team may have the role of standardizing product messages (that's usually the Marketing Department). Each team's role will help the organization achieve its mission, as discussed in Chapter 6. And before you can assign individual roles, it's important for everyone to understand how their team functions in the larger, interrelated, organizational eco-system.

Once the team's role has been clarified, you're ready to assign individual roles to your team members. We use the word *assign* loosely, as there are many ways for it to happen: an employee may volunteer for a role, or her manager may actually assign it. Someone may suggest a role for a colleague (*"Jose is good at this,"* or *"Magdelene does that faster than anyone else"*). Someone may get stuck with a role because no one else is doing it. Or somebody may slip into a role because it's what he did at his last job. In spite of all these *ad hoc* assignments (which almost always come into play), it's part of your job to try to manage the role assignment process in a way that's best for your team, and best for each person—with the team's input, if you can.

With roles so critical, and the assignment process so complex, you can see why getting buy-in for people's roles is so important. If an employee has been *"volun-told"* for a role, or has accepted his role half-heartedly, there will eventually be problems with the way she performs the tasks associated with that role. Similarly, if the employee (no matter how well-meaning) doesn't understand the full commitment level necessary to fill the role he's been assigned, you're heading toward confusion, resentment, and, possibly, a UE situation. So as you explain the "assigned" roles to each of your employees, discuss them in a way that motivates the employee and creates buy-in.

Then document each role in a way that can be used to confirm expectations, to referee disputes, and to create accountability when needed. Don't assume that everyone will correctly remember his or her exact role. Without a specific write-up to refer to, you're likely to wind up with duplicated efforts, overstepped boundaries, and gaping holes.

Finally, in addition to clarifying roles, **The Roles Diagnostic Chart** can also help you diagnose problems. If your team continues to grapple with role issues, check how the roles were assigned or accepted. And if there is enthusiastic buy-in for roles, yet employees are still asking questions such as *"Who do I talk to?"* or *"Who approves this?"* look at your documentation for guidance and brief your team on their roles again.

Solution

Blaine decided that he would try to clarify the subject of roles in their practice with Ian. So he shifted some assignments, freed up some of his and Ian's time, and invited Ian into his office. Blaine even bit his tongue when the first thing Ian did on arrival was flop down on Blaine's "kiddie couch" and toss his blue-jeaned leg over the arm. It occurred to Blaine that Ian had *a lot* to learn about acting professionally!

Blaine also realized that Ian was nervous (though Ian was trying to hide it with a casual slouch) and that they would have to get to the point quickly. Don't hesitate to jump right in: Your UE knows that you've called him in for a reason, and he isn't going to be able to concentrate on anything else you say until you've told him what that reason is.

Blaine: *Ian, I'd like to talk with you briefly about something important.*

Ian: *Sure. What's up?*

Blaine: *I don't know how to say this except to just say it. I got a complaint about you this week from a parent who said you weren't giving her the medical information she needed.*

Ian: *Are you talking about Jen Latrelle's mother? I never met a more uptight woman in my life!*

Blaine: *Well, I wish I could tell you she's the only person who's spoken to me about this, but she's not. This is actually the third complaint I've had in just the last four weeks.*

Ian: *Are you serious?*

Blaine: *Yeah. Unfortunately, I am.*

Wisely, Blaine paused here to let Ian take in what he was saying. Few people like to hear that their work performance is considered a problem, so give them a little time to absorb the bad news. And be prepared for the possibility that your UE may try to turn the conversation back on you, with a comment like, *"I can't believe I'm just hearing this now!"* or *"Why didn't you tell me there was a problem?"* Confirm that you're hearing the comment, but don't forget that this conversation is about the UE, not about you. Don't go along with a change of direction, either by agreeing (*"You're right. I stink."*) or disagreeing (*"Well, you're hearing it now, so get over it!"*). Just wait quietly, with your face neutral, until your UE responds to the real issue.

With Ian, this happened pretty quickly. After carefully searching Blaine's face (and not seeing any emotion, or way out), Ian sat up straight, and looked more thoughtful. This was the cue that Blaine had been waiting for to know that Ian was ready to hear more. Blaine paused a bit, then continued the conversation.

Blaine: *Ian, can I ask you a question that might sound a little obvious?*

Ian: *Yeah, I guess so. Sure. What is it?*

Blaine: *Well, how would you describe your role in this practice?*

Ian: *What?*

Blaine: *I said it was going to sound obvious!*

Ian: *Yeah, you did. I'm a pediatrician. A staff doctor. My role is to serve my patients and maintain a good working relationship with you and the other doctors.*

Blaine: *Okay. Are there any important constituents missing from that description of your role?*

Ian: *Yeah, now that you mention it, the office staff and nurse practitioners. They play a big part in keeping the kids healthy, too.*

Blaine: *How about the parents? Can your patients, the children, stay as happy, healthy, and strong as possible if their parents aren't actively on board?*

Ian: *No, of course not.*

Blaine: *So how would you describe your role in relation to the parents?*

Ian (doing a Sherlock Holmes imitation): *Elementary, my dear Watson. My role is to help their kids get better.*

For a second, Blaine was torn. He wanted to point out that what Ian had just done (slipping into his Joker attitude during a serious conversation) annoyed Blaine and threatened Ian's credibility. On the other hand, he and Ian were moving down an important path, and Blaine didn't want to get sidetracked.

"You Pays Your Money and You Takes Your Chances"

Every turn in every conversation is the equivalent of a multiple-choice quiz. Do you respond to the other person's words, or to his or her tone? To what is actually being said, or to what you think the other person means? Do you mention your own reactions, or not? Press your point, or move on? Repeat yourself, or let it go? There's no way to know what approach will work best. Just pick a strategy, and take your chances. If it doesn't work, try something different.

Blaine: *So let me ask you: Is helping their kids get better your only role with relation to the parents?*

Ian: *I don't get what you're asking.*

Blaine: *Do you have any direct role with the parents themselves?*

Ian: *Sure. Keeping them informed.*

Blaine: *Anything else?*

Ian: *Answering their questions?*

Blaine: *Anything else?*

Ian: *Well, I try to help them keep their spirits up, just like I do with the kids. But I have to tell you, I don't think they really get it. Some of them have no sense of humor, like Mrs. Latrelle.*

Blaine made a quick decision to break out of questioning mode.

Blaine: *Ian, can I share a personal reaction? A minute ago, remember when we were talking and you went into your "Sherlock Holmes" voice? I was actually quite annoyed by that.*

Ian: *You didn't like my imitation?*

Blaine: *I didn't like feeling that you might not be taking me seriously.*

The casual way that Blaine delivered this feedback helped Ian hear it as a confirmation of other people's reactions (like Mrs. Latrelle's) rather than an attack on his humor or style. It's often the case that an unpleasant message is easier to hear and absorb if it's delivered in a truthful and matter-of-fact way.

Ian: *Wow. I'm really sorry. That's not what I meant at all, but I guess what you were bringing up made me nervous.*

Blaine: *Sometimes you joke around when you're nervous?*

Ian: *Not with the kids. I'm never nervous with them. But some of their parents are pretty daunting. Pushy, hysterical—you know the drill.*

Blaine: *What do you think those parents are feeling?*

Ian: *I suppose some of them are nervous, too. I know Jen Latrelle was in the ICU for a few days last week. I guess her mom's got a good reason to be upset.*

Blaine: *How could you help Mrs. Latrelle handle that?*

Ian: *Well, probably not by being The Joker....*

Blaine: *You don't have to give him up. The kids love your sense of humor. But I think the parents would be happier with you in the role of trusted advisor.*

Ian: *I guess I could do that. Kind of like playing the responsible big brother. That way I could still be myself, but tone it down for the parent conferences.*

Blaine: *That sounds to me like it would work.*

Ian: *All right. I see your point. I'll try to change my act with the parents.*

For Ian, who loved play-acting, the phrase *change my act* showed that he was ready to embrace what could have been a threatening challenge, and turn it into a chance to have fun. His theatrical bent was also the reason why Ian literally pictured a dramatic character, the "responsible older brother," when he was reconsidering his role. Not everyone makes up characters, though; your UE might go through an entirely different thought process to arrive at a new and improved role he can embrace.

And remember that, just as people visualize or understand their roles differently, they also may have very different reasons for gravitating toward the roles they do. Ian was playing The Joker because (a) he loved his patients, and (b) he hadn't thought carefully about his role in relation to their parents. But *your* UE's clowning around might come from a very different motive, such as rebelliousness, boredom, or even a fear of adult responsibility. In these cases, the conversation that you have with him will be very different from the one Blaine had with Ian.

Result

At this point, Ian had agreed there was a problem, accepted the clarification of his role with respect to the parents, and agreed to "change his act" and apply his love of joking more appropriately. When Blaine thought later about this conversation, he realized that he'd met his goal of *discussing* (**Step 2: Communicate**) and *solving* (**Step 3: Clarify**) the problem with Ian in one conversation.

After some thought, Blaine saw that Ian did not need **Step 4: Coaching** (his attitude was fine), and over the next few months the changes he made demonstrated that that he was able to **Create Accountability** (**Step 5**) for himself.

As you can see, some of **The 5 Cs** can take longer than others to execute, depending on your particular UE and situation. There is no set rule for the amount of time you should apply to each of the framework's five steps. What's important is that you go through **The 5 Cs** systematically, one at a time, in order. This will take the guesswork out of your process, and allow you to focus on your UE instead of having to wonder what to do next. When your UE senses that you are truly *committed* to her as an individual (which you will decide in **Step 1** and communicate in **Step 2**), she is more likely to respond to your efforts—particularly when they're backed up by the full force of your attention.

Chapter 7 Summary

» *Unclear roles can create unmanageable and unruly situations.*

» **The 10 Communication Questions** *will help you plan the key points to discuss with your UE.*

» *Use* **The Roles Diagnostic Chart** *as both a starting point and a problem-solving tool to help you define, assign, get buy-in for, and document the roles on your team.*

» *Understanding the team's role within an organization will help employees understand their individual roles. Once they understand their role, be sure that they have accepted the role and understand the commitments that are necessary to fill it.*

Hot Tips	
If your UE says...	Try responding with...
"It's not my problem if people have no sense of humor."	"Lack of humor is your perspective on them. What do you think is their perspective on you?"
"What do you mean, people have been complaining about me!? Why am I only hearing this now??"	"You seem upset. I get it. But let's stay on track, because these complaints are important."
"Tell me who complained. I've got a thing or two to say to them!"	"That's not relevant to this conversation. How do complaints impact our team?" (NOTE: A manager should never give names.)
"Why can't I just work with the people I'm good with? Why do I have to deal with everyone else, too?"	"Teamwork is vital. What's your role on the team?"

◇◇

The Joker

"Is there any room for individuality in this organization?"	"Each person has individual talents. What are your best assets?"
"This is a stressful job. I need to let out steam somehow!"	"How can you do that without negatively impacting the team?"
"You're just out to get me because I'm young, old, brown, white, male, female, etc."	"This isn't about personalities. This is about performance. How would you honestly rate your performance during the past six months?"

The Do-Gooder

You've seen that there is no magic formula for salvaging a UE, and no standardized benchmarks to apply. But we hope that, by now, you and your UE are at least beginning to forge a sense of common purpose. The faster you can align with your UE around eliminating unmanageable behavior, the more smoothly UE salvage will go.

As you learned in the previous chapters, clarifying roles is an important part of that effort. Confusion about roles can result in misplaced efforts and damaged relationships. It can also result in responsibilities not taken—or taken for the wrong things—which is what happened with our next UE.

Meet The Do-Gooder

Having a Do-Gooder on your team can be a huge bonus. Do-Gooders are often personable team players who are liked and appreciated by one and all, and who want to help their colleagues and team succeed. In general, Do-Gooders listen well, make time to interact with (and support) their peers, are empathetic, and pay attention to the niceties at work, like thanking people, buying birthday cards, even helping to plan the holiday party when you don't have time to do it. They always seem to know the right thing to say or do, in every situation.

Unfortunately, there is one key ingredient missing in the Do-Gooder's recipe for success, and that ingredient is balance. Balance is vital to an organization's success at every level: Just as the management team must balance revenues versus expenses, or weigh the value of giving an assignment to one person vs. another, employees also perform a constant balancing act as they try to reconcile their limited time with ever-expanding priorities and workloads. Often, however, a Do-Gooder doesn't know *how* to balance his workload and say no to time-consuming requests from other people. As a result, his time can be eaten up by the personal demands (and dramas) of colleagues, and a formerly positive Do-Gooder can descend into overload, missed deadlines, and unmanageability.

Case Study: Everyone's BFF, Bella

In addition to being a senior project manager, Bella was her construction firm's go-to person for team morale. As everyone's unofficial "best friend forever," she was the bringer of cookies and kind words—the person who constantly looked for ways to help others. Whether their problem was professional or personal, everyone counted on Bella for advice, assistance, and moral support.

Problem

When Jeremy, a newly promoted 27-year-old manager, became Bella's boss, he liked her immediately. Her warm personality and dedication to the team were definite pluses in his mind. On the other hand, Jeremy was concerned that Bella often failed to meet her own responsibilities. Clearly, she was capable of doing her job and meeting Jeremy's expectations; in his opinion, she fell short because of the time and attention she gave to others.

Jeremy wanted Bella to get her own work done first, and help other people only *after* that. But two things made him second-guess that goal: First, he didn't know how to respectfully criticize the behavior of someone who was twice his age; and second, he didn't want to lose the positive contribution that Bella made to team morale. He was glad to have an employee who showed so much enthusiasm when she came to work each day, and he wasn't sure that she fell into the category of unmanageable—even though the situation that she was creating clearly did!

What's in a Name?

Don't waste time wondering whether your UE is "truly unmanageable," "technically unmanageable," or "just barely unmanageable." If you think **The 5 Cs** can help you manage your UE better, jump in and try it; don't worry about the labeling. And remember that, although there are truly unmanageable employees—people who delight in causing trouble, cheating the system, and creating pain, dysfunction, and chaos—it's unlikely that your UE is one of them.

"C" Stands for "Balance"

Jeremy decided to see if **The 5 Cs** could help him restore some balance to Bella's job performance. He also hoped that going through the steps would help him clarify how to best manage her.

Step 1: Commit or Quit

When Jeremy used **The "What's it Worth?" Worksheet** to calculate the costs and benefits of retaining Bella, he was able to affirm his gut-level decision that Bella was an asset to his team. This exercise helped Jeremy commit to working with Bella for the next six months, after which he would reevaluate the situation.

Step 2: Communicate

Given Bella's open and congenial personality, Jeremy felt that talking to her about the problem would be relatively easy; but it turned out he was wrong. When he first raised his concerns to her, Bella brushed them off, saying, *"I like to work with people who are happy, so I take the time to help them feel that way."* At first, Jeremy was discouraged by this, but he pushed himself to bring it up again, and the next time, Bella listened more carefully to his comments. After gentle prodding on Jeremy's part, she finally admitted that playing "Do-Gooder" to the whole team was negatively impacting the quality of her work.

Step 3: Clarify Goals and Roles

All of this brought them to **Step 3**. When Jeremy thought about Bella's role, he quickly realized that she actually played *two* roles at their construction firm: her official role as a senior project manager, and her unofficial role as the team's morale booster. It seemed to Jeremy that the lack of balance between those two roles was causing Bella's performance issues, and he couldn't wait to find out if she agreed.

Can clarifying the balance between roles really change a UE's behavior? Yes, and Bella is a case in point! Like many (perhaps the majority of) unmanageable employees, Bella knows that what she's doing at work doesn't quite pass muster. But she'll need guidance—and a way to understand why what she's doing isn't working—so that she can succeed at managing the work on her plate.

The Balance Tool

One of the ways to help a UE understand why she's not succeeding is by showing her **The Balance Tool**. This simple diagram helps managers and their UEs visualize how well or poorly the UE is balancing her competing work roles and priorities. Because it's so visceral and easy to grasp, this tool is perfect for introducing a conversation about your UE's choices, and about whether a different balance would be better for her, as well as for others. Jeremy did that in the following conversation:

Jeremy: *Bella, what would you say if I suggested that you actually have two main roles here at work?*

Bella: *I'd say, "Of course I do. A project manager has 20 roles!"*

Jeremy: I *didn't mean just as project manager. It seems to me that your second role is helping the entire team feel good.*

Bella: *You're right, of course. I'm very proud of doing that.*

Jeremy: *I know, and I'm torn about it, because—in that unofficial role—you do a lot for the team. And we've already talked about your work not getting done. There must be some way that both things can happen.*

He then took out **The Balance Tool,** and explained what it represented.

Jeremy: *Trying to balance our various commitments at work is like balancing a scale, or a see-saw. If you put too much weight on one end, the other side becomes too light, and can even seem to float away. So tell me: If you look at this picture, which of your two roles do you think gets more weight?*

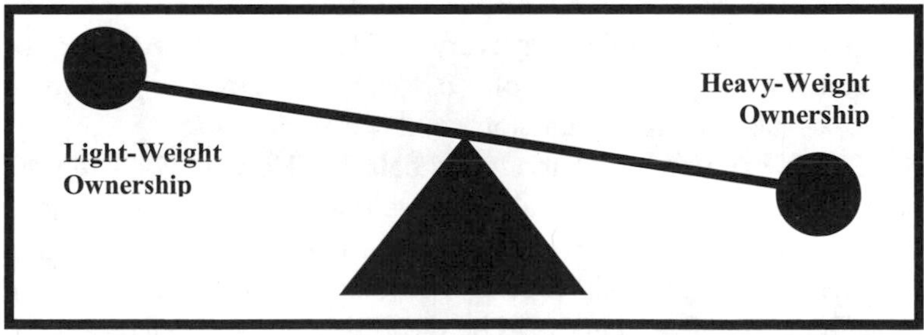

Bella studied the diagram for a minute, while Jeremy waited patiently. Finally, she said:

Bella: *Truthfully? I guess in my heart, the real challenge I come to work for is helping other people do their best. My actual job duties are okay, but I don't feel the passion for them that I feel for making the team run well.*

Jeremy: *Thanks for sharing that with me, Bella. That's what I thought was going on.*

At that point, Jeremy was in a delicate position. On the one hand, if he came down on Bella by demanding that she curtail the role she enjoys, he would damage their relationship, and her commitment to the team. On the other, if he didn't begin to move her toward change, he'd be neglecting his own responsibility to make sure his team members did their jobs.

What's a manager to do?

Keep the Fire Burning

When an employee is passionate and motivated at work, he is more likely to succeed. And most people would agree that being passionate also gives one a sense of satisfaction, even power, that helps people overcome workplace challenges. Yet, passionate employees can become unmanageable employees if their passion and enthusiasm are misplaced or take away from the performance of their primary roles. Think of the employee who focuses on tasks that are peripheral to your team's goals. Or the one who's passionate about pursuits such as organizing a sports betting pool. Or the person whose passion is for following every rule to the "T," whether or not any actual work gets done. All of these employees may be passionate *at work*—but they're not passionate *about their work!*

So how do you find that needed balance? How do you keep the fires of passion burning, yet also ensure that your UE does her job? It starts, during **Step 2: Communicate**, with getting your UE to agree that her passion is actually causing a problem. As Jeremy saw, this can be difficult; but if you persist, as he did with Bella, you will be able to make your case. Then use **The Balance Tool** to visualize where your UE's energy is going, and talk about the impact that this energy allocation has on the team's (and your UE's) success.

Another Delicate Crossroads

Now here comes the tricky part. Although you may want to support your UE (and all your employees) in getting what they need to be fulfilled, your first responsibility is to the company's mission and goals. So your overall objective is not about employee satisfaction—it's ultimately to direct the UE's passion into areas that will help your team and your organization move forward successfully. Here's how Jeremy discussed this with Bella:

Jeremy: *Bella, I've been thinking about your unofficial role of Do-Gooder. I know you feel strongly that this role helps people keep a positive attitude, and helps the team run better.*

Bella: *Yes, I really do feel that. I've tried to cut back since we've been having these conversations, but I wouldn't want to stop helping other people completely.*

Jeremy: *I agree that you're bringing value in that role. But the cost, when your projects are behind, is too high. How can we resolve this issue?*

Bella: *Realistically, I don't know. But the more I think about this situation, the more I wish I'd gone into Human Resources. That seems to be where my real talents lie.*

Talk about a balancing act! Jeremy was now in the position of having to balance Bella's needs against his own, and those of his organization. At that point, he could pretend he didn't hear what was just said (something most of us are occasionally tempted to do, when a comment opens a can of worms). He could agree that it was too bad Bella missed the HR boat, but that she was a good project manager so it's probably for the best. Or he could hear and acknowledge the importance of her comment, and begin to think about whether Bella's words indicate a possible solution to their problem. Because Jeremy knew that listening to Bella and taking what she'd said seriously was critical to maintaining her trust, that's what he did.

Did it make sense to consider shifting Bella's official responsibilities? Jeremy didn't know the answer, but he decided to talk to his boss and find out. Although he didn't like the idea of losing her as a project manager, it was now clear to both of them that Bella was much more vested in her *unofficial* role than in the one she was being paid to fill. Because she didn't have an HR background, Jeremy wasn't sure if the company would allow her to make a move to that department, but his instincts were telling him to at least explore this path.

Stay Open to Your Intuition

Not everyone believes in intuition or gut instinct, but most of us recognize that, sometimes, answers come to us when we least expect them. In fact, it can be counterproductive to sit at your desk and brood about what to do with your UE when you're feeling too burned out to concentrate. Whether or not the idea of intuition appeals to you, you may sometimes feel the need to put a problem aside and sleep on it, or come back to thinking about it later when you're fresh. That's not surprising, because managing people (with all their complexities) often requires creativity. And creativity often sneaks up on you when you least expect it—when you're watching a movie, hanging out with friends, or, yes, even sleeping. Try to stay open to any insights that come to you, no matter how strange they may initially seem. Often, breakthroughs appear odd at first, but then begin to make more and more sense. And who knows: A fresh angle, a new thought, even a gut feeling or hunch may turn out to be just what you need to help you solve the stubborn problem your UE is presenting.

Solution

As it turned out, the company was willing to try out shifting the balance of Bella's roles. At Jeremy's suggestion, the company's owner agreed to offer her a part-time, interim, entry-level HR role to see if she liked working in that area. The key would be getting Bella's buy-in, as Jeremy made clear when he took the idea to her:

Jeremy: *I've been talking to the owner about giving you a part-time, interim position in HR. There are a couple of caveats, though. If we give you a part-time project management load, you'll have to keep your projects on budget and on deadline. And if you decide that you prefer HR, you're going to need some training in that area.*

Bella: *Jeremy, that's fantastic. I can't believe you did that for me!*

Jeremy: *It's not an unconditional offer. You'll have to be an exemplary project manager, and it's going to be even harder to balance your workload while you're learning a new skill. Do you think you'll be able to do it?*

Bella: *I'd like to try. A lot of the time I spend looking after everyone else can be folded into my HR duties, right?*

Jeremy: *Well, that's what we're going to have to see, and we'll create a system to hold you accountable for your duties in both departments. I don't think it'll be easy, but if you are committed to this, then I'll support you. This is a chance to create a win-win, and if you're willing to take responsibility, I think we should go ahead and try it.*

Bella was thrilled with this idea, and they started to plan in detail for the transition.

When Your Entire Team Needs to Change

As our case study illustrates, an unofficial role can cause unmanageable situations, because, when an employee has adopted such a role, enjoys it, and is good at it, she's unlikely to *want to* change. An astute manager will therefore broaden the lens to look at his or her entire team or department, asking:

- *What roles are required for success?*
- *Which ones are currently unfilled?*
- *Who is the best person to fill each role?*

When there's a real need for the UE's unofficial role—a need that would go unmet if the UE suddenly reformed—it may be preferable to legitimize the UE's *unofficial* role by making it her official one, and assigning her former role to someone who will perform it more diligently. Of course, this is *much* easier said than done. It takes time, wisdom, and determination to pull off such a realignment. People may have to be shuffled, and the organizational chart re-created. Is it impossible to do this? *No.* Is it way more work than a manager "needs"? *Yes!*

◇◇

The Do-Gooder

And even when an employee is moved into a role that's theoretically a better fit, there's still lots of work to be done, because it's rarely the case that the people on your team and the roles available for them will match perfectly. Do your best to put each employee in a role that she can grow to fill over time. If, for example, your UE fits a new role 80 percent of the way, but needs help with, say, customer relations to make it to 100 percent, don't discard her like an old tennis shoe. Give her the role and help her improve her ability to perform it through training and/or coaching.

Results

Jeremy was able to create a new role for Bella. That isn't always possible, but there's usually *something* you can do to balance a UE's role more closely with her particular interests and enthusiasms. It might be placing her on a committee or subcommittee, letting her mentor others in her area of strength, or giving her special assignments that keep her passions engaged while serving the team. It's well worth looking for solutions that will strengthen your UE's enthusiasm for her job, even if that means shuffling some roles. Just be sure that, whatever you decide to do, you have the employee's buy-in before moving ahead.

Chapter 8 Summary

» **The Balance Tool** *lets employees visualize how well they are balancing competing priorities, and determine if that balance needs to change.*

» *A frank conversation with your UE will reveal the relative weight and passion she gives to the different roles she is playing. If possible, find a way to direct her enthusiasm toward a role that supports the organization's mission; or find a way to reshuffle roles so that she can bring more passion to her job.*

» *Be sure your UE takes responsibility for whatever role she agrees to play. This will help her gain more power and a higher level of respect from her colleagues, and motivate her to succeed at work.*

Hot Tips	
If your UE says...	Try responding with...
"Why can't I do what I want to do in my free time?"	"How would that help the team move forward?"
"No one appreciates all the good things I do for this organization."	"What contributions would you like to be more recognized for?"
"I'm fulfilling my job description. Why do you suddenly want more?"	"What exactly is your job description?"
"Are you trying to stifle the creativity I bring to my job performance?"	"How can your creativity help us solve this problem?"
"I like taking care of other people, and it makes the work go better for everyone."	"How does your desire to help others impact your performance?"
"I'm the best employee you've got. You should appreciate that and leave me alone."	"You're part of a bigger team. How would you describe our team's current performance?"
"That's how I am. I can't change, and I don't want to."	"When can change be a good thing for our organization?"

The Wallflower

As you've seen in previous chapters, UEs can become unmanageable for a wide variety of reasons. Sometimes they don't understand their role in an organization. Sometimes they don't realize how their behavior is perceived by others. Sometimes, though, they just have a negative *attitude*. And that is a very, very big problem. Along with knowing *how* to do his job, and having the resources he *needs* to do his job, nothing impacts an employee's job performance like his *attitude* toward the job!

As you saw in **Chapter 5**, if your UE has a dismissive attitude toward members of her *team*, she can turn your office into a minefield of hostility and resentment. And if your UE has a challenging attitude toward the *organization* or its goals, that can undermine his performance and your entire team's success, as you saw in **Chapter 6**. But as you know, troublesome attitudes—just like UEs—come in all sizes, shapes, colors, genders, cultures, and styles.

And they aren't always directed *outward*. For many managers, the most difficult kind of UE to manage is the one who *could* be doing better, *should* be doing better, but *isn't* doing better because he just doesn't believe in his own capability. What do you do when your UE suffers from a bad attitude toward *himself*?

Meet The Wallflower

Wallflowers are often overlooked—particularly in large organizations—because of their quiet manner and lack of self-promoting bravado. When managed well, these shy employees can add tremendous value to a team. But if they're managed without regard to the special challenge their unassuming natures poses, they can quickly turn into UEs.

Your time is a precious commodity, and too often it goes to the "squeaky wheels"—your more outgoing employees or UEs. The challenge that your Wallflower presents is: How do you build his (or her) self-confidence, while also doing everything else that you need to accomplish in a day? This can be a daunting task. The skilled manager knows, however, that if she can bolster her Wallflower's self-confidence, this former UE will sparkle and shine.

Case Study: Training the Animal Whisperer

As a skilled and experienced veterinary technician, Jung had earned the respect of his colleagues; and because of his animal skills and know-how, his manager, Ilyana, recommended him for a supervisory position. Unfortunately, it soon became clear that Jung's profound hesitancy, his ambivalence about his new role, his avoidance of anything that might cause conflict, and his chronic procrastination might keep him on the sidelines of career success.

Problem

It's natural for a manager to promote her skilled and dedicated employees. Retaining knowledgeable and effective people is vital to a team's success, and giving them room to grow and develop is a key part of any manager's job. Yet sometimes an employee doesn't have as much confidence in himself as the manager has in him. That's when a situation that should be positive, such as a promotion or increased responsibility, can turn into an unmanageable one, as it did in the case of Jung.

The first day of Jung's supervisory training did not go as well as Ilyana had planned. Although he could clearly handle the work, Jung seemed unsure of himself. Even his "animal whisperer" technique was off that day, but Ilyana just chalked it up to nerves. She figured that Jung would feel more confident in a few days.

During the week that followed, Ilyana kept asking Jung to create a new schedule for his direct reports. One of them was going on maternity leave, and Jung would have to make sure in advance that her shifts were going to be covered. Although this was a routine supervisory job, Ilyana and Jung both knew it would cause a lot of grumbling. As Jung continued to put this task off, Ilyana began to worry that he might be defeated by his fear of how other people were going to react.

The 3 A's: Attitude, Aptitude, Available Resources

As Anne described in her previous book. *A Manager's Guide to Coaching,* employees must have "The Three A's" to succeed: They need the *aptitude* (relevant skills) to perform their jobs. They must have enough *available resources* (including equipment, time, and support). And they need to have an effective *attitude*, including the internal confidence, drive, and focus to overcome challenges and persevere. Attitude, which can seem like the least tangible of The Three A's, has traditionally presented the greatest challenge to managers.

Sometimes it can take considerable effort to uncover a UE's attitude issues. (In **Chapter 10**, you'll learn how to do that.) But with other UEs, their attitude problem is right on the surface for all to see. Here are some examples of employees who have the skills and resources to do their jobs, but have clearly lost the attitude that's essential for them to succeed:

» *In the past, Joceleyne's sales meetings had been models of speed and efficiency, but now, her meetings regularly ran over time. When someone asked her about it, Joceleyne replied, "Whatever. What's 10 to 15 minutes between friends?"*

- *Lila used to teach the "Communications 101" course to more than 100 people, without a hitch, and to invariably rave reviews. But her current course, using the same material and technology, is receiving comments like, "Average at best," and "Not sure I'd recommend this class to a colleague."*
- *Nabil, a wedding planner, knew how to plan a wedding reception in his sleep while keeping both sides of the family happy. His latest clients weren't happy, however, because Nabil spent more time texting in the kitchen than tending to the needs of the bride, groom, and guests.*
- *Iris had been making successful presentations to her small team for years. Her manager counted on Iris for top-notch graphics and content, and Iris felt confident and proud in front of her team. Yet when she was asked to make a presentation to the board of directors, Iris made excuses about why she wasn't able to do it.*

Of course, you may not automatically be able to see these bad attitudes. Sometimes a manager is too involved, or standing too close to the situation. In that case, you might miss the obvious and decide that a UE is underperforming because he's lazy, or doesn't care. You might think she's not following directions because she has a problem with authority or disrespect for the organization's goals, or because she doesn't like you personally. Before you buy into any of these theories, be sure you've considered the possibility that your UE *has a poor self-attitude!* Ilyana could easily have concluded that Jung didn't really *want* a promotion when, in reality, his own *self-doubts* were pushing him to the brink of failure.

It's surprising how often this happens. You've probably heard that the stress created by a positive change, such as a promotion, is just as intense (and difficult to manage) as the stress created by negative changes like a death or serious illness. Getting promoted is a big deal, and no matter how skilled your employee is, she'll probably feel at least *some* self-doubt when she thinks about the challenges ahead. That's why it's always wise to have a frank conversation about your employee's concerns and questions up front, before giving her a host of new responsibilities. (If she says she has *no doubts at all*, ask her if she really means that!) A candid conversation of this sort will do much more than just clear the air. It will help you create an effective training program to address any areas of weakness that your employee brings to her new position. And even more importantly, it will demonstrate that you truly want her to succeed.

Don't Forget The 5 Cs

The 5 Cs can help a manager handle *any* UE, including those with confidence issues. So even if you've diagnosed *attitude* as what's causing your UE's unmanageability, be sure to work through all **5 Cs** to verify your thinking and choose a course of action. Sometimes this process will be time-consuming, but sometimes it can be done quickly. Either way, it's vital to take all the steps, as Ilyana did:

» *Ilyana had implicitly completed* **Step 1: Commit or Quit** *when she helped Jung become a supervisor, even though she knew his areas of weakness. Granted, she hadn't expected the self-esteem issue to become so challenging, but she still felt confident that helping Jung succeed would bring far more benefits than costs.*

» **Step 2: Communicate** *went quickly, as well. Jung named the problem himself, telling Ilyana, "I'm not sure I'm supervisor material." They both knew that he had the skills and resources to do the job; the problem was his own negative attitude toward himself.*

» *In terms of* **Step 3: Clarify Goals and Roles**, *both Jung and Ilyana knew what his future role would be: supervisor.*

Ilyana realized that the place to begin her UE salvage operation was with **Step 4** of **The 5 Cs: Coach**. When Ilyana thought back, she realized that she'd expected Jung to be thrilled when she told him that he was being promoted. Instead, he'd replied with *"I'll give it a shot, if you want, but I'm not sure I can do it."* Ilyana still believed that Jung could do it, and her question was: *How can I help him grow into that role with as little disruption and discomfort as possible?* She was ready to help her animal whisperer whisper some courage into himself!

Acknowledge, Don't Praise

After talking to her supervisor, Ilyana settled on the strategy of using acknowledgments to help Jung develop more confidence. *Acknowledgments* are a powerful coaching tool for recognizing and encouraging an employee's growth in a particular area. This quick practice—not to be confused with *praising*, as we'll explain—helps an employee feel seen, heard, and valued. Often spoken (rather than written) and specific (rather than general), acknowledgments strengthen and empower employees by giving them fact-based validation.

As an employee (UE or otherwise) grows into new skills or responsibilities, acknowledgments can be particularly powerful. The idea is related to positive reinforcement, but rather than being a "feel-good technique," as some managers fear, acknowledgments are the equivalent of a *verbal progress report* that allows you to direct an employee's growth by commenting, in an appropriate and credible way, on her efforts, successes, and strengths as she moves toward achieving her goal.

It sounds simple, and yet acknowledgments can be a hard skill for busy managers to learn. Part of that is resistance to soft skills, but some of it is just not knowing how to say the words. To give an effective acknowledgment, you must do the following three things:

1. Catch Your Employee Doing Something Right

Okay, be honest! How often do you see an employee doing something well, and neglect to mention it? And how often do you see the same employee doing something wrong, and immediately comment? Most managers would answer, "Usually" to both those questions. And that's not surprising, given that your focus is improving employee performance.

But if you only point out an employee's mistakes, you're training him to *expect criticism* every time you open your mouth.

You probably remember someone in your life—a relative or neighbor or grade-school teacher—who never noticed the good things you did, and only criticized you for the bad, right? How long did it take you to tune out that person, and ignore *everything* he or she said to you? That's how people generally respond, but fortunately, there is no need for you to use negativity as a management tool. As the old saying goes, you'll "catch more flies with honey than vinegar"—and motivate more employees that way, too. That's because positive reinforcement *works*. And the key to making positive feedback a cornerstone of your effective management technique is simply to catch your employees doing things right, and then tell them, in specific detail, what you saw!

2. Look for Areas of Progress

As you practice "catching your employee doing things right," look in particular for behaviors that indicate *areas of progress or growth*. Most of us enjoy positive words, but those words can be especially sweet when they recognize the specific ways that we're working hard to improve our performance.

When an employee stretches his comfort zone, when she responds to constructive feedback, when he takes a risk or achieves a milestone, that's the time for an acknowledgment. And remember: An *observant* acknowledgment trumps an elaborate acknowledgment every time. Something like *"Hey Jack, I saw you stand your ground at the meeting today. That's new for you,"* will surprise Jack, and help motivate him to keep standing his ground in the future.

3. Be Specific, Objective, and Matter-of-Fact

When you do acknowledge progress, be sure to make your comments objective. (The example about Jack is a case in point.) Seems simple enough, right? But it's not. Most managers *praise*, instead of giving an acknowledgment, and there's a big difference in the impact of each.

151

There are several key differences between praise and acknowledgment, as the following chart makes clear.

- **Praise** *is general;* **acknowledgment** *is specific.*
- **Praise** *gives you the power to judge;* **acknowledgment** *just reports what you observe.*
- **Praise** *can be extravagant;* **acknowledgment** *is matter-of-fact.*

Here are some examples of praise along with a corresponding acknowledgment:

Praise vs. Acknowledgment	
"That was a great report!"	"I can see that you spent a lot of time on the report. It's much more detailed and analytical than your previous ones."
"Nice job at today's meeting."	"I saw you speak up at today's meeting with a clearly outlined plan for next week's press conference."
"People loved your presentation today."	"I heard that your graphics in today's presentation were clear and compelling."
"You did an awesome job with the team."	"I noticed that your facilitating style allowed everyone to make their point in the allotted time."
"You're doing a fantastic job."	"You've made steady progress in achieving your revenue goal this month."

As you can see, although an acknowledgment is measured and objective, it's much more personal and impactful than praise. That's because praise is often given quickly, without thought. Praise could apply to many people, but because of its specific and precise nature, an acknowledgment can only be about *the specific person you're talking to.*

◇◇

The Wallflower

152

Make Your Acknowledgments Real

We've stressed that acknowledgments are objective; but don't make them dry, detached, or robotic! No matter how perceptive your acknowledgment, if you give it in an indifferent tone of voice, it's not going to achieve the goal. Remember: Acknowledgments work because they make people feel valued. The key is to mean what you say, which you will if you follow these steps:

» *First, notice what your UE did right.*
» *Use the* **Acknowledgment Checklist** *to pin down what you observed. Don't get hung up on the exact wording; the fact that you noticed is what counts!*
» *Practice, by giving your employees regular acknowledgments. The more frequently you do this, the less of a challenge it will become.*

How do you know if your acknowledgment was heard? Just watch the response you get! If your UE nods absently and mumbles "Thanks" or "Whatever," you can be sure that you either gave him praise (which can often sound insincere), or delivered your acknowledgment in a less-than-engaged way. If he straightens up a bit, looks you in the eye, or smiles with pleasure, chances are good that you aced the acknowledgment.

Acknowledgment Checklist	
What did I observe my employee doing right? (Be specific.)	
How is this different, or how does this represent progress, for him or her? (Be specific.)	
Did his or her action produce a positive effect? (Be specific.)	

Acknowledgment Checklist	
When will I tell him or her about this?	(Hint: What's wrong with now?)

The **Acknowledgment Checklist** will help you create the desired effect. When you feel an acknowledgment coming on, answer the questions in the left-hand column. And notice that *any* time is the right time for an acknowledgement. (Okay, maybe not *any* time. But it's difficult to find the wrong time for something like this.) Every employee, not just your UE, can benefit from hearing acknowledgments; And that's good, because you probably need to practice giving them. So don't wait for the "perfect" moment—jump in and give it a try.

When you do this for the first time, you may notice a funny reaction (like, *Hey, why is she being so nice to me?*). This reaction could be verbal, if the UE blurts out the actual words, but it might also be conveyed nonverbally, by a puzzled, surprised, or skeptical look. Either way, don't backtrack into praise to avoid the employee reactions, because once your employees realize you mean it, they'll be motivated by the fact that you've seen (and acknowledged!) their efforts to grow. And remember: The more specific an acknowledgment is, the harder it will hit home. Your employee will know exactly what behavior was effective, as he grows into his new role.

Solution

Throughout the next week, as she continued to train Jung for his new position, Ilyana took care to point out Jung's strengths *in dealing with people* through acknowledgments. (She focused on the interpersonal because it was an area where Jung needed to grow, as opposed to building his confidence around the animal skills that he already knew were solid.) Here are some examples of how she did it. Notice how thoroughly they differ from a general comment like, *"Jung, you're doing great!"*

» *When Jung handled a client request well, she said, "I saw how you made direct eye contact with Mrs. Clark. She seemed confident that you were taking her needs seriously."*

- *After Jung handled a tense moment with Moses, the most assertive of his soon-to-be direct reports, Ilyana remarked, "You spoke to Moses in a quiet, calm voice. He lowered his own voice when you did that."*
- *Before Jung went to lead the first meeting of his new team, he showed Ilyana his meeting agenda notes. She told him, "These notes are clear and concise. You seem to have put a lot of time into preparing them."*
- *After much nudging from Ilyana, Jung finally started to create the staffing schedule that he'd been putting off. It still needed much work, which Jung admitted. But Ilyana said, "I know how hard this was for you to start. The staff's response could be negative, yet you overcame the fear of making people mad, and did it anyway. That takes strength and self-confidence."*
- *When Jung finally presented his new schedule to staff, he started out by asking them to support their colleague on maternity leave. The team agreed that they would try the new schedule for the next 6 months. Jung was visibly relieved that there was no animosity displayed at the meeting. Ilyana commented, "You could have presented that schedule in many different ways. Asking for their buy-in and consensus brought the team together."*

Result

Every time Ilyana gave Jung an acknowledgment, she noticed that, afterward, Jung spoke up more often and seemed more enthusiastic about his new role. She knew that he needed more supervisory training, and that she would have to continue investing her time and attention to develop Jung before he could *truly* feel comfortable running a team. Yet Ilyana was encouraged by his progress, and glad to see that her unmanageable Wallflower was finally beginning to trust himself.

Building a UE's self-confidence takes time, practice, patience, and the ability to put your focus on the employee in front of you. In the course of your busy day, the easiest thing in the world is to overlook a Wallflower and focus on your squeaky wheels. We get that, and yet we strongly urge you to take the time to catch your employees doing things *right*. You'll be pleasantly surprised by what you find—and your UE will be gratified that you're commenting positively on her efforts. As you develop your own skill in giving acknowledgments, strive to give at least one each day, until it becomes an ingrained habit. (Acknowledge yourself for doing it!) The time it takes to give an acknowledgment will be well-rewarded as your Wallflower, and other employees, grow stronger and more self-confident.

Chapter 9 Summary

- *Sometimes UE behavior can be caused by a lack of confidence, or poor self-image. The best way to handle this is through coaching with acknowledgments.*
- *An acknowledgment is a form of positive feedback that strengthens and empowers employees by giving them fact-based validation.*
- *Praise is different from an acknowledgment. Praise is general, can be applied to anyone on the team, makes a judgment, and disempowers the employee (because you hold the power to praise, or not).*
- *Use the* **Acknowledgement Checklist** *to help you think through what you'll say:*

    1. *Catch your employee doing something right.*
    2. *Look for areas of progress.*
    3. *Be specific, objective, and matter-of-fact.*
    4. *Give the acknowledgment as soon as you can.*

Hot Tips	
If your UE says...	Try responding with...
"I'm not sure I can do this, but I'll try it if you want me to."	"How can I help you be successful with this?"
"You promoted me? You must be really hard up!"	"I see potential in you. What do you see in yourself?"
"If I start telling people what to do, they're all going to hate me."	"Good managers listen and ask questions, instead of telling people what to do. How can you use questions to lead your new team?"
"I can't do this! I just don't have what it takes."	"You're struggling now. I get it. Let's break this into smaller steps."
"I'm just not the leadership type."	"What does a successful leader look like to you?"
"It was nothing. Anybody could have done what I did."	"What will it take for you to accept credit for a job well done?"
"You do realize that promoting me was a mistake, don't you?"	"What makes you think it was a mistake?"

10

The Gossip

You've seen how effectively the **Acknowledgment Checklist** can help you build a UE's self-confidence. Sometimes, though, self-confidence isn't the issue! Like Ruby (The Egomaniac in **Chapter 5**), a UE can feel fine about herself, yet hold attitudes toward other people that lead to unmanageable, team-crippling behavior.

That's where **Coaching Questions** come in. You have no direct control over your UE's attitude—but by asking questions that make him think, you can *influence* not just his attitude, but how he expresses it in his behavior. When your UE needs to find the inner motivation to improve his behavior, **Coaching Questions** will often do the job.

Meet The Gossip

Let's face it: Gossips can be entertaining. They often provide a welcome distraction from the daily grind, and they don't appear to do much harm.

After all, The Gossip isn't generally malicious, and the person who's being gossiped about doesn't *know* what's being said about her—right? Wrong! Gossip is a verbal virus that can infect your team just as surely as the most virulent flu. Whether it spreads slowly or like wildfire, gossip will weave itself into the fabric of your organization, and weaken the threads that hold your people together.

Case Study: Max Versus the C-Suite

Max isn't just a world-class gossip; he's a master at sowing the seeds of discord. Not only does he waste time and effort trash-talking everyone on his team, but he also seems to have a special knack for spreading the kinds of rumors that demoralize people, and turn them against each other. His favorite form of gossip, however, is attacking people in the C-Suite with personal comments that diminish their authority and "bring them down a peg."

Problem

Julia, Max's manager at the Internet broadband company where they both worked, was becoming very concerned about Max's repeated tendency to loudly and proudly knock the top brass. People were starting to avoid Max—and who could blame them when his "conversation" increasingly consisted of irrelevant comments such as:

- *"The CFO's house is so over the top! Who was his designer?"*
- *"I guess our CMO thinks he's worth that big paycheck he's been getting."*
- *"The COO's children are running wild again. Can you believe that, last week, she actually had to bail her youngest son out of jail?!"*

Julia was particularly distressed by these comments, because they showed that Max was abusing his position. Because Max was a senior manager and Julia was a VP, they both had access to the private lives of the organization's C-level executives. Clearly, Max was going too far in sharing that information with others.

Because she'd always liked Max, Julia checked in with another VP, Peter, to see if her instincts about Max's gossip were off-base. *"Max's gossip is a liability to the team,"* he said. *"No one wants to be around him anymore. It's becoming a real problem."*

Why Gossip Matters

Many managers are concerned about gossip, but wonder if they're overreacting. After all, isn't gossip just a harmless way for employees to blow off steam? Should they really be taking it so seriously? The answer is an emphatic *yes*—because, at its core, gossip is *a commitment to failure*. Gossip kills trust, motivation, and integrity. It can kill the fabric of an organization.

Does that sound alarmist? Think of it this way: Jack and Jill may be climbing the hill, but if Jack is talking about Jill behind her back, isn't Jack silently, secretly hoping that Jill will come tumbling down? In other words, that she'll fail in some way? And if Jack is hoping that Jill will fail—even though that would weaken the organization—how committed can he really be to the success of the entire team?

Sometimes, though, gossip is not an individual matter. When gossip is widespread and not coming from just one UE, it indicates a more serious problem that can only be addressed by *open and honest communication from the top*. This means communicating by actions as well as words. If your employees are gossiping about a possible merger, counter that by holding informational meetings and sharing as much as you prudently can. If they're gossiping about potential layoffs, try to resolve their concerns transparently. Widespread gossip often indicates a troubling information void. Most people need to understand where they stand and what the status of their organization is before they can feel secure at work; so be sure to fill that void if you can.

Get the Advice You Need

Julia took her colleague Peter's warning to heart. She was convinced that Max posed a problem that had to be solved, before the gossip spread. Her only question was how to go about it; so she sought the advice of her mentor, Fred.

Fred reminded Julia about a management seminar they had both taken several years before that focused on using **coaching questions** to improve employee performance. *"I remember that,"* Julia said. *"But how do I coach someone about gossip?"* Fred replied, *"Get Max to see how gossip is getting in the way of* his *success. There's no better motive for changing behavior than wanting to improve your own success."*

What's in It for Me (WIIFM)?

Like all the rest of us, UEs are motivated by self-interest. This means that, counter-intuitively, the very behaviors that seem to an outsider to be least adaptive and most self-defeating are, by definition, providing some kind of payoff to the unmanageable (otherwise, she would stop doing them). Though it's not your job to figure out what that payoff is, you need to keep this dynamic in mind, because it explains the incredible persistence of self-defeating patterns. In fact, we've probably all experienced how annoying, infuriating, and counter-productive it can be to get "well-meaning advice" from someone who doesn't realize that we're stuck in bad behavior for a reason, no matter how flawed or inadequate that reason may be.

Why Coach?

Julia dug out her seminar notes to be sure that coaching was her best choice. She quickly confirmed that when a UE's problem seems related to *attitude*, rather than *aptitude* (mastery of relevant job skills) or *available resources* (support from the organization)—coaching is the recommended way to proceed. If your UE lacked job skills (aptitude), you could help him increase his skills through training. And if your UE lacked organizational support (available resources), you could give him a hundred times more resources. You could even order him (a hundred times!) to give the gossip a rest, but none of these actions will change his behavior, because the problem is his *attitude*.

Coaching is the number-one tool to improve attitude (including focus and self-motivation) because attitude is an "inside job." This means that the issues represented by inappropriate attitudes lie deep within the employee herself. Training and resources can't touch them; in fact, effective coaching questions are not just the best, but the only way to help a UE think deeply about what's *really* going on. Coaching brings a UE to awareness, and then action. And you need both of those elements to succeed.

- *Awareness without action is like navel-gazing, or sitting around a campfire holding hands and singing "Kumbayah." Everyone may feel great, but nothing much is getting done.*
- *Action without awareness leads to tail-chasing, or jumping head-first down a rabbit hole and wondering why you keep hitting your head. Plenty of stuff is getting done but none of it is particularly effective.*

How to Ask a Coaching Question

The hard part of coaching a UE is asking questions that work to inspire awareness and action. Managers ask questions all day; however, a coaching conversation requires a *different type of question*—the type that allows your UE to do *his own best thinking* about his problem.

How do coaching questions accomplish this? In general, the ones that work best share three characteristics: They are open-ended, advice-free, and short.

1. Good Coaching Questions Are Open-Ended

Because they allow for yes-or-no answers, *closed* questions tend, by their nature, to close people down.

On the other hand, *open-ended* questions, which usually start with the words *what* and *how,* encourage candor and discussion. This is important because, for an employee to change her unmanageable behavior, she needs to participate in defining the problem, recognizing its impact, and seeking a solution. (Attitude problems, as noted before, almost never yield to "orders to change.") Imagine how well the following exchange between Julia and Max would work:

Julia: *Max, you like to gossip a lot, right?* (Closed question)

Max: *I guess you could say that.* (Translation: yes)

Julia: *Are you aware that this is a problem*? (Closed question)

Max: *I don't think it's a problem.* (Translation: no)

Julia: *Well, it is. Do you know why you act like that?* (Closed, judgmental question)

Max: *Who knows?* (Translation: no)

Julia: *Well, for the good of the team, will you cut it out, please?* (Statement/direction phrased as a question)

Max: *Sure, Julia. Whatever you say.* (Translation: no)

In this example, the questions were short, but they had no other noticeable virtues, and they certainly didn't succeed in engaging Max's interest or curiosity. It's a pretty good bet that Max would quickly forget the discussion once he walked away, along with his "promise" to curb his gossip. Yet these questions could easily be transformed from **closed** to **open-ended**. Here are some examples of the difference between the two:

Closed vs. Open-Ended	
"Do you see how this is hurting the team?"	"What impact do you think this has on the team?"
"Are you ever going to stop gossiping?"	"What motivates you when you need to change a behavior?"
"Why are you gossiping about her?"	"What's the reason for the gossip?"

The only caution about using open-ended questions is to be sure that there is *no blame* involved. *"What's wrong with you?"* may be an open-ended question that begins with *what*, but it will never start a productive conversation!

2. Good Coaching Questions Are Advice-Free

If you want to coach effectively, it's important to avoid questions such as, *"Have you thought about X?" "Why don't you try Y?,"* or *"What's wrong with doing Z?"* These "questions" are really thinly veiled statements that pressure the UE to take your advice. Of course, most managers *want* to give advice. They got to a higher position in the organization because they know how to get things done, and they believe that their advice will help an employee get things done, too.

Unfortunately, the one thing that advice from a well-meaning manager *can't* get done is to drive a change of attitude within a UE (or any other employee). That's why a savvy manager asks advice-free questions such as:

- *"What are some other ways to think about this?"*
- *"What's the underlying problem?"*
- *"How do you see this playing out?"*

This chart compares "questions" that are really just advice in disguise with comparable advice-free questions.

Advice-Filled vs. Advice-Free	
"Don't you want to stop gossiping?"	"What would happen if you stopped gossiping?"
"Have you decided to change yet?"	"What would changing this look like?"
"Wouldn't you be more successful if you stopped acting like this?"	"How do you define success?"

◇◇

The Gossip

3. Good Coaching Questions Are Short

If you ask a lengthy question or a complex one that combines two or three different thoughts, it's easy for the person you're questioning to slip through the cracks of your logic and digress or to just answer the easiest part of what you've posed. Asking short questions lessens that possibility and frees you from having to manage several lines of discussion at once. So make your coaching questions short (preferably eight words or less) and on point (with just one idea at a time). Here are some examples of short, focused questions (along with their opposites):

Long vs. Short	
"If you had to describe the impact of gossip on your team, and had to explain how you plan to stop it, would you be able to answer that? And what answer would you give?"	"What would be the first step to stopping the gossip habit?"
"In what ways do you think this gossip is contributing to your reputation? And is that reputation congruent with where you see yourself being in this organization two years from now?"	"Where do you want to be in two years?"
"Why do you think that you gossip, and what does your assumption about the underlying cause of your behavior say about your ability to make a change, particularly in the near term?"	"What's the underlying reason?"

The Qualities of UE Questions

As noted good coaching questions should be as **open-ended, advice-free**, and as **short** as you can make them. These qualities are important for coaching any employee, but they're critical for your UE.

This is because you want your UE to *think for herself*, and **open-ended** questions promote that. You also want to lower the emotional temperature and prevent any defensive reactions to your feedback, which you'll do by sticking to **advice-free** questions, rather than offering unwanted advice. Finally (and frankly), you don't want to give a UE any wiggle room, and **short** questions are the way to avoid that.

With non-unmanageables, two other qualities of general coaching questions are forward-focus and thought-provoking. But UEs often aren't ready to think about the future. They have issues that must be resolved in the present before they can start to think long-term. So don't worry about asking them **forward-focused** questions; it's better for you to focus on what's going on now. And whereas it's also true that you want your UE to *think*, you want him to think about becoming less unmanageable—not about the more theoretical, long-term options that are generally raised by **thought-provoking** questions.

To learn more about this topic, see Anne's first book, *A Manager's Guide to Coaching* (American Management Association, 2008; written with Brian Emerson).

Solution

Armed with these insights, Julia scheduled a conversation with Max. Because she suspected they would be talking multiple times—it often takes multiple conversations with a UE before you start to notice a change in behavior—her first goal was to see if Max had any *awareness of the problem*, and to help him become aware of it if he wasn't. Their conversation went as follows:

Julia: *Max, this may not sound work-related, but humor me, okay? What's your opinion of gossip?*

Max: *Gossip is harmless fun. Light entertainment. Everyone does it. I even do it from time to time. It's no big deal.*

Julia: *It may seem like no big deal to you. However, I've gotten three complaints about your gossiping from three different people, including a C-level executive.*

Max: *Three people? Really? How can that be? I don't gossip that much! I think they're just overreacting.*

Julia: *You know, I started paying more attention to your language after I received those complaints, because I also thought people might have been overreacting. But I noticed three comments that I would call gossip at Monday's meeting, and two more at the meeting today. I jotted down what you said, to show you.*

Max: (reviews Julia's notes) *I do remember saying those things, but I didn't think anyone was listening. You're right. I did say that stuff.*

Julia: *The fact that I've gotten three complaints seems like a problem for both of us. Fielding them takes away from my work. And you being viewed in that light could potentially take away from yours. Would you agree that there's a problem?*

Max: *Yes, I guess I would.*

Max was surprised to learn that Julia *listened* to what he had been saying in meetings, but listening is a crucial skill that all good managers work to master. You've heard of the 80/20 rule, right? Twenty percent of your clothes get worn 80 percent of the time. Eighty percent of the meals you eat out are eaten in 20 percent of the restaurants you go to. It's possible that this formula has no scientific validity at all, but it crops up all over the place because it feels intuitively right to people. We all know that some large portion of our activities (let's say, 80 percent) cluster around a small portion of the available options (let's say, 20 percent) and so we recognize this as one of those intuitively correct propositions.

To coach well, any manager needs to apply a variant of the 80/20 rule: **Listen 80 percent of the time, and speak only 20 percent of the time.** Why? Because you want to create an opportunity for the UE to do his own best thinking during the coaching session. If you're doing most of the talking, the UE has much less chance to think for himself. Ask powerful coaching questions that elicit responses, and then be sure you *listen* to what your UE says.

167

3 Levels of Awareness

In her first conversation with Max, Julia was able to move him to **problem awareness**, meaning awareness that there *is* a problem. It can be hard to get a UE to admit this, and there's no magic formula for success. Your best bet is to listen, and ask short, open-ended, advice-free questions. No matter what happens, keep trying, because your UE can't solve his problem until he becomes *aware* of what it is!

The next challenge in coaching a UE is moving him toward **impact awareness**. Often UEs are so self-focused that they don't realize the effect they're having on the people around them. This myopia can change by helping the UE gain an understanding of the consequences of his behavior. Often (though not always), when a UE sees the impact that his behavior is having on others, he begins to think about changing it.

At that point, half the battle is won. But how do you create impact awareness? One way is by asking the million-dollar question: "*What's the impact of that?*" This powerful question allows the UE to think for himself about how he's effecting his team and organization. Remember that the goal of coaching is to *help your UE find his own answers*. You're not telling him; he's figuring it out for himself. In the process, he'll start to own the solution, which is what happened when Julia moved Max from awareness of the problem to impact awareness:

Julia: *Max, last time we spoke, you agreed that people's complaints about your gossip was causing a problem for both you and me. Today, I want to ask you: What's the impact of gossip on the person being talked about?*

Max: *Not fun, probably. Maybe they'd get mad. Perhaps embarrassed. It could make them distrustful.*

Julia: *What's the impact of working with someone you don't trust?*

Max: *The team won't gel or produce. Something like that could split the team in two. I suppose the person who's gossiping might get excluded or shunned by everybody else.*

Julia: *You told me in our last conversation that you think gossip is harmless fun. Yet you just said that gossip could potentially split the team in two, or make it not gel. So how harmless is gossip?*

Max: *I guess not very.*

At this point, Max had agreed there was a problem (**problem awareness**) and admitted that his behavior was having a negative impact on himself and other members of his team (**impact awareness**). He was now ready for the third—and most important—level of awareness: **self-awareness**, or awareness about the thinking or motives behind his behavior. Julia felt ready to coach Max toward this new milestone. But, to her surprise and disgust, Max kicked off their next meeting by making a sneering comment about their CEO's lack of fashion style.

Julia wanted to start yelling, *"Haven't you heard a word that I've said???"* Fortunately, she remembered in time that this wouldn't be considered a coaching question! So she went to get a glass of water, and came back with her perspective restored. The next time she coached Max, Julia started with a simple question:

Julia: *Max, what does gossip get you?*

Max: *What? What are you talking about?*

Julia: *Well, like what you said about the CEO's clothes. You've already said that gossip is a problem. And then, when we talked last week, you were able to describe its impact on the team. (pause) Everyone does things for a reason. What was your reason for the comment you made?*

Max: *Julia, I'm just trying to let off some steam!*

Julia: *But there are lots of ways to do that. What are some other reasons to gossip?*

Max: *All right. Maybe I'm jealous of the CEO.*

Julia: *What are you jealous about?*

Max: *She makes about 10 times more money than I do, and she spends it all on clothes that look bad. If I had that money, I'd know how to spend it.*

Julia: *So maybe bringing her down a notch?*

Max: *I don't think that's why I do it.*

Julia: *Okay. But it's doing something for you. Will you think about what that is? I'm looking forward to your answer.*

The next day, Julia and Max happened to cross paths at the company cafeteria. When they sat down to talk some more, Julia was determined to keep her questions at a high level. Sometimes focusing on the minutiae of a situation creates a never-ending circle of accusations and defensive words. When this happens (and also when you've had a breakthrough), bring the conversation up to 30,000 feet and ask a related macro-level question. This changes the dynamic, and allows both the UE and you to focus on the bigger picture. That was Julia's goal when she picked up her conversation with Max:

Julia: *Did you figure out what gossip gets you?*

Max: *I did think about your question, and I'm embarrassed to say that I realized I am jealous of the C-level salaries. So I like making those people more "human" by telling stories about them. And it keeps my day interesting.*

Julia: *Thanks for being so honest. That's not an easy thing to admit. Max, what made you join this company?*

Max: *What? What does that question have to do with gossip and what I just said?*

Julia: *I'm curious. What was it that first attracted you to this place?*

Max: *I loved the idea of working with a dynamic team, creating new tech products that could change the face of the Internet.*

Julia: *You were on fire when you started. And as we discussed the other day, your gossip can create distrust and split a team. How does that impact your performance?*

Max: *I may be splitting my team without realizing it. But I don't think so. They're strong.*

Julia: *They are strong. And they could be stronger. I want you to watch your team closely this week and see what impact your gossip is having on them. We'll talk about it next week.*

The next week, they met in Julia's office and had the following conversation:

Julia: *How did your homework go?*

Max: *Not so well. It was kind of sobering. When I really paid attention to each player on my team, as well as the team dynamics, I saw that you were right: They're not as strong as they could be. And once I gossiped by mistake and you could see Paulo's reaction. He stopped looking me in the eye and left quickly after the meeting. I asked him later that day why he left so quickly; he said that he enjoyed working with me, but not when I was putting down other people. He thought the gossip denigrated me and the team. I've never been spoken to like that before.*

Julia: *Powerful feedback. That's a lot to digest. What do you want to do with this?*

Max: *I don't want the people on my team to be thinking bad things about me. I want to stop this gossip before my team implodes. Or explodes. Or whatever.*

Julia: *How can I help?*

Max: *I don't know yet. I need some time to think about it.*

Julia: *Fair enough. I'll circle back with you in a few days.*

When she did, they had this conversation:

Julia: *When we last spoke, you were committed to changing your gossip behavior. What ideas have you come up with?*

Max: *Nothing. I'm stumped. I didn't even know it was an issue until you brought up those three complaints, which led to my conversation with Paulo.*

Julia: *What's important to you?*

Notice what Julia just did. Because Max didn't have any useful ideas at the micro level, she once again shifted to a 30,000-foot view, with a provocative question about his macro goals. Remember that you can always take a conversation up (getting more "macro," as Julia did), down (more "granular"), or sideways (into a related topic). Although it's important to keep your UE focused on the problem at hand, it also pays to shake things up sometimes and bring in a fresh perspective. After all, one of the things your UE's behavior reflects is his inability to think creatively about whatever troubling situations he finds himself in.

Max: *What do you mean, "what's important to me"? Is that another one of your weird questions?*

Julia: *I'm serious, Max. I want to understand you better. What's important to you in your life?*

Max: *My teenage girls. Security. Innovation.*

Julia: *How would you feel if your teenage daughters started gossiping about you and the things that happen in your home?*

Max: *I wouldn't be happy about it.*

Julia: *I'd like you to think about what you would do to help them stop, if that's what you wanted. Let me know tomorrow what you thought of, okay?*

Often a UE sees the impact and truly wants to change a behavior, yet doesn't know how. It's now your job to help him find a solution on his own, so that he doesn't fall back on his old habits. Once your UE is ready to change, keep asking questions until he creates his own process for doing so.

The next day, Max sought Julia out with a reaction to the question she'd asked him.

Max: *Got a minute?*

Julia: *Sure.*

Max: *I thought about your question. If my daughters started gossiping about me, I'd see it as a sign of disrespect.*

Julia: *You're doing the same thing. You're disrespecting the senior people of the organization. You secretly want them to fail.*

Max: *That's harsh.*

Julia: *Is it true?*

Max: *I just want to take them down a notch and make them more human, not make them fail.*

Julia: *Max, we're going around in circles. I want you to think about whether or not you're really willing to change this behavior.*

The Elephant in the Room

What Julia was doing when she flagged the contradiction in Max's attitude is sometimes called "naming the elephant in the room." The phrase *elephant in the room* refers to our tendency to tiptoe around even the most obvious truth, if it's uncomfortable for us to confront it. Examples of an elephant in the room might be a conversation about employee morale in which no one mentions that half the workforce was fired the week before; or a meeting to plan strategy for Q2 in which no one mentions the big loss your organization took in Q1, or even (on a more positive note) a discussion about possible locations for the company's annual meeting in which no one notes that, once again, you'll probably go to Aspen because that's where the CEO likes to ski.

Given the amount of denial and avoidance that goes on in everyday life, you won't be surprised to discover that stating reality can be an important and useful coaching tool (because reality has an important place in all good coaching conversations). In fact, during the coaching process, it's not unusual to name the elephant in the room, or state the obvious about a situation, in a matter-of-fact, non-judgmental way. This helps the employee see what she's been avoiding or procrastinating on.

Naming the elephant in the room might not be your best starting position (remember that the goal is to *let the UE solve his own behavioral problem*, not for you to mention that there's a 2,000-pound pachyderm sitting on his right leg). But at some point, naming the elephant in the room may help your UE recognize reality, admit that his circulation has been cut off, and commit to a course of action that will change things for the better.

Julia truly didn't know, when she arrived at work the next day, if that was what would happen. She could imagine Max finally making a commitment to change, and offering a concrete plan for how he would stop gossiping. But she could also imagine Max reacting negatively to the whole process, and trying once more to justify his behavior. Julia hoped it wouldn't be the latter! When they got together, later in the day, she held her breath while Max opened the dialogue:

Max: *I thought about what you said. You're right. I want to take the top brass down a notch. I'm not a team player with this attitude.*

Julia: *It sounds like you're now aware of the thinking behind your behavior. That's not easy to admit. And no, you haven't been a team player. What are you going to do about that?*

Max: *I can help build the team by stopping my gossip.*

Julia: *How will you do that?*

Max: *Well, I'll need your help. Here's my idea....*

Result

After that conversation, Julia and Max worked productively to help Max drop his gossip habit. If Max still gossiped a little during their meetings, Julia reminded him that his gossip was disrespectful and pushing the organization to fail. Julia also gave Max positive reinforcement through acknowledgments (as described in **Chapter 9**), which helped Max see his progress over time. In addition, she held weekly meetings with him, to discuss the moments when he had a hard time keeping his gossip under control. These conversations helped Max increase his own self-awareness of which situations could potentially trigger gossip in the future. All of this helped Max change his behavior for the better, and helped Julia build a stronger team.

Was it time-consuming? *Yes.* Was it easy? *No.* Did Max stop gossiping completely? *No.* But he *was* able to curb this habit most of the time, thanks to Julia's coaching questions and techniques.

Is the Cure Permanent?

Because nobody is perfect, a salvaged UE will likely go back to his comfort zone of unmanageable behavior when she's under stress. Keep alert to this possibility, and continue to coach her and give acknowledgments when this happens.

Chapter 10 Summary

- *Gossip kills, and is a commitment to failure.*
- *Coaching can help UEs fix their own behavioral problems.*
- *An effective coaching question is* **short**, **advice-free**, *and* **open-ended**.
- *In order to change their behavior in the long-term, UEs need to have three levels of awareness:* **problem awareness**, **impact awareness**, *and* **self-awareness**.

Hot Tips	
If your UE says...	Try responding with...
"Talking about people doesn't hurt them."	"Gossip hurts team morale by creating a negative environment. What are the impacts of working in a negative environment?"

Hot Tips	
If your UE says...	Try responding with...
"Gossip is a universal, human thing. Aren't we supposed to be human around here?"	"How would you react if you knew that your trusted colleague was talking about you behind your back?"
"Why are you asking me all these crazy questions?"	"These questions help you and me understand each other's perspectives better."
"Why don't you focus on someone who has a real problem instead of hassling me?"	"Gossip is a real problem, especially for the person being gossiped about. How can gossip become a problem over time?"
"Don't you ever talk about anybody else?"	"What's the difference between talking about someone behind his back and to his face?"
"Well, people talk about me behind my back, so why shouldn't I talk about them?"	"What are the long-term impacts of an organization that encourages gossip at every level?"
"No one's perfect. Why can't you let a little thing like this go?"	"Gossip kills trust and collaboration. It's not taken lightly in this organization."

11

The Slacker

Congratulations! You've worked hard, and your UE has made tremendous strides. Now it's time to lock in those gains, and minimize the chance that they'll erode over time due to inattention, pressure, or "just because." For **Step 5: Create Accountability**, you'll need a tracking system that helps both you and your former UE keep your eyes on the prize of ongoing high performance.

Meet The Slacker

Although *slacker* is a word that's sometimes used as a slur against younger generations, in reality, it has nothing to do with the age of your underperforming UE—it simply refers to your UE's work habits (or, more precisely, his lack thereof). How do you spot a Slacker on your team? Just look for the person who does the bare minimum of work. The person who never volunteers for any additional duties. The person who has a "laissez-faire" attitude about meeting his goals (and that's putting it kindly). When you find that person, whatever his age, you've identified your team's very own UE Slacker.

Case Study: All That Glitters Is Not Employee Gold

Despite his charm, skill, and good looks, Stephen was only an average manager. He let his team do whatever they wanted, rarely spent any one-on-one time with them, and was barely achieving his own goals, let alone the goals for his team. He often left work before his employees and arrived later than them each morning. He told his superviser, Julio, that team members kept "bothering" him with questions. Julio had heard through the grapevine that Stephen's team didn't like working with "The Little Prince."

Looks Can Be Deceiving

Psychologists have long known about the "halo effect," which causes most people to project a wide range of desirable qualities onto people that they find attractive. But your most personable and attractive employees are not necessarily the most productive. Use concrete, tangible measurement systems to rate your employee's actual performance. This will give you an accurate read on each employee's success rate and value to the team.

Problem

As the newly appointed senior manager of an IT team, Julio had started out being impressed with his direct report, Stephen. Stephen seemed to be good at everything; he was bright, handsome, and charming, and seemed to have been in the right place at the right time for his entire life. An excellent computer jock, he was also a gifted salesman. Every time he interacted directly with a corporate client, Stephen managed to upsell something.

What a disappointment, then, when Stephen turned out to be at best, an underachiever, and at worst, a dead weight. On his previous job, Julio had successfully used **The 5 Cs** to salvage an unmanageable employee. He was curious to see if they'd work with Stephen, too.

The 5 Cs in Action

Julio decided to give himself four to six weeks to work through **The 5 Cs** with Stephen (assuming that **Step 1** came out "**Commit**"!). Here is what happened when he did:

» **Step 1: Commit or Quit**. *Using* **The "What's It Worth?" Worksheet**, *Julio determined that, if Stephen could become more productive, he would indeed be a valuable member of the team, due to his tech talents and sales experience. So Julio decided to* **Commit** *to a salvage operation.*

» **Step 2: Communicate**. *Julio began by giving Stephen his feedback on the problem. Unfortunately, Stephen didn't agree with Julio's analysis; Stephen thought his work habits were just fine. It wasn't until Julio showed Stephen the agreed-upon goals and current performance levels that Stephen admitted his team wasn't going to achieve its quarterly goals.*

- **Step 3: Clarify Goals and Roles**. *This was a difficult one. Stephen understood the organization's goals, yet did not want to accept his team's role in achieving the organization's mission. He only really started to listen when Julio helped Stephen see that the organization's success was directly related to Stephen's bonus. This was a small step forward, but Julio still found it discouraging.*
- **Step 4: Coach**. *After Stephen's failure to grasp the importance of* **Step 3**, *Julio knew that* **Step 4** *would be his last chance to salvage his UE. The series of conversations they had became a turning point for Stephen.*

The first little chink in Stephen's armor came when, during one conversation, he was able to articulate (for the first time) that things weren't going *quite* as well as he liked other people to think. Julio gave Stephen plenty of time to let that small admission settle in. In their next conversation, Stephen astounded Julio by saying that he'd been thinking hard, and that it *was* true that he had coasted on the backs of others most of his life. Julio was fit to be tied. He'd been close to giving up on Stephen several times, and he'd begun to doubt that his UE would *ever* reach that point of clarity.

Through Julio's ongoing coaching (which took the form of short, open-ended, and advice free questions, "casually" dropped into quiet moments), Stephen gradually became curious about how it would feel to succeed in a job through nothing but his own hard work. He told Julio that he didn't know how to succeed through work instead of charm!

From Insight to Accountability

Stephen had now reached the third level of awareness that's needed for any UE to change. He had admitted there was a problem (**problem awareness**), faced the impact it was having (**impact awareness**), and examined his own motives and capabilities (**self-awareness**). It was now possible for Julio and Stephen to create an action plan that would help Stephen develop the **aptitude** (capabilities) needed to successfully manage others.

In a way, they had come full circle: Stephen had talent, contacts, and personality; what he didn't have (and clearly had never had before) was someone holding him accountable. What would happen, Julio wondered, if he actually required that Stephen meet his goals? It seemed to Julio that **Step 5: Create Accountability** was his best hope for turning this UE underachiever into a valuable manager and member of the team.

What Is Accountability?

Accountabilty simply means *holding someone responsible for his commitments.* It would be natural to assume that, if someone's made a promise, he will try his best to keep it; but often, even with good intentions, our best efforts are not good enough. This can happen for reasons that range from illness or a work crisis to personal struggles like self-doubt, procrastination, or lack of discipline. Often, people most need to be held accountable when they try something new. For example:

> *A top CEO decides to write a book, which she knows will take time. She's confident that she has the writing skills to pull this project off, but is less sure about her ability to carve time out of each busy day throughout the long period required. So she finds an accountability partner—someone who agrees in advance to hold the CEO to her commitment—and promises to write a chapter each week.*

Knowing that her accountability partner will actually ask for that chapter each Friday makes it much more likely that the CEO will make the time to do her writing instead of putting it off.

Remember that accountability does *not* mean "blame." In fact, it means just the opposite. If you hold your UE accountable for clear metrics on a regular basis, you eliminate the need to accuse, harangue, or say angry things like, *"You were supposed to do this!"* Because both people have agreed to the commitment, the conversation can be calm and reasonable. You can simply say, *"We agreed that you'd complete the report today by 5 p.m. I'm looking forward to seeing it."*

Accountability Is a Two-Way Street

We know what your UE is accountable for, but what are *you* accountable for, as his manager? This is an important question. If your UE agrees to do something by a certain date, but you, his manager, fail to hold him accountable, what happens?

First, your UE knows that you're not tracking his goals. Second, your UE concludes that you probably won't track his goals carefully in the future, either. As a result, your UE slips rapidly back into unmanageability. (Remember, if your UE was good at regulating himself and his behavior, he wouldn't have become unmanageable in the first place.) So, yes, *you are accountable for maintaining his accountability.*

At this point, many of our clients rebel. They say, *"Wait just a minute! I worked hard to get to this point. Why do I have to keep track of* his *commitments, too? I have my own problems to track. He's a grown man, let him act like one!"* It's hard to argue with this point of view, so we don't. We just ask, *"Are you willing to take the risk of losing what you've gained so far?"* Usually, that answer is no. And it helps to know that this won't last forever. After a while, you'll be able to spend less time checking on your UE's goals because *he will begin to do it himself.*

Reminders

As hard as we try to remember it all, most people get tied up with other things, and can easily forget until a deadline or important conference call is upon them. The same is true for a UE, especially one who is trying to create new behaviors. So give your UE a reminder, one or two days before the deadline. Keep your reminder simple and focused: "Hey Morgan, I'm looking forward to seeing your research in two days." If the UE has the situation under control, that's great. And if the UE is behind on his commitment, your comment will help him to gear up while he still has time to meet the deadline.

What Does Accountability Look Like?

Without strong accountability, it's unlikely that a UE will be able to clean up his act for any length of time. But before you can create accountability, you and your UE must agree about exactly what he's accountable for. Be sure to check your mutual understanding of these five items:

1. *What is being completed?*
2. *When will it be completed?*
3. *Who will it be delivered to?*
4. *Where will it be delivered?*
5. *How will it be delivered?*

Let's look at each of these in detail:

What is being completed

You and your UE must be crystal clear about *what the end product of his commitment looks like*. Vague ideas won't work here; the more specific you can be, the better. Is the deliverable a conversation with someone? A meeting? Research on a particular topic? A report?

And if what you *really* want is "a 10-page report that discusses X," say so! Don't just call it "a report." For one thing, that's not enough direction. For another, you won't have a leg to stand on if your UE delivers something that's "too short."

When will it be completed?

What is the agreed-upon date and time for completion? Again, the more specific, the better. So get clear about (and state!) whether "*Tuesday*" means "*9 a.m. on Tuesday*" or "*close of business on Tuesday*." (And what does "close of business" mean?) In addition, create benchmark dates along the way, to ensure that progress is being made.

Who will it be delivered to?

Who needs to see the final product? Just you? A client? Other people?

Where will it be delivered?

Where exactly does the end product need to go? If the deliverable is going to a client, does it go to her headquarters? His local office? His hotel room at a conference? His home?

How will it be delivered?

What is the methodology that will be used? Snail mail? E-mail? Overnight delivery? Face-to-face? Fax?

Making the Intangible Tangible

Most accountability agreements involve a tangible product, such as a report, memo, e-mail, or phone call. But, as you'll see in **Chapter 12**, you can also create accountability for less tangible commitments such as thinking about an important topic, or holding a difficult conversation. Even if the deliverable is intangible, make your expectations specific by asking who will be in the conversation, when it will happen, and what the desired outcome will be.

The Accountability Tracking Tool

To create an objective record of whether or not your UE is meeting his agreements, use **The Accountability Tracking Tool.** This tool is a simple chart that promotes agreement with your UE by putting expectations in writing. It gives you an overview of check-ins and deliverables. And it reminds you to track your UE's goal, and keep him accountable for his commitments.

The Accountability Tracking Tool can also help you monitor goal metrics for all of your employees, not just your UE. You'll be pleasantly surprised at how easy it is to implement this tool across your department, and use it for your entire team.

The Accountability Tracking Tool (Fill out for each agreed-upon deliverable.)					
Deliverable	**Benchmark Dates**				**Comments**
What is being completed?					
When will it be completed?					
Who will it be delivered to?					
Where will it be delivered?					
How will it be delivered?					

Solution

Julio knew that implementing a new accountability system with his Slacker UE would have to be done slowly. He wanted to be sure this system didn't overwhelm either one of them by giving them both time to work out the kinks. For now, they agreed to focus on only one of Stephen's overdue goals: updating the sales revenue program so that multiple sales managers could enter data at the same time. Julio filled in **The Accountability Tracking Tool** to reflect what he and Stephen had agreed on:

The Accountability Tracking Tool (Fill out for each agreed-upon deliverable.)					
Deliverable	Benchmark Dates				Comments
1. What is being completed? Update the sales revenue program so that multiple sales managers can enter sales data at the same time	1/15	1/30	2/15	3/1	-need to review current program -need to get input from all sales managers on current problems, what would like to see, how often do they update sales info?
2. When will it be completed? Final deliverable: March 15					-create weekly benchmarks -check team's schedule—how to fit this into their workday?

The Accountability Tracking Tool (Fill out for each agreed-upon deliverable.)					
Deliverable	Benchmark Dates				Comments
3. Who will it be delivered to? Julio and Hamza, the sales manager					-check if CFO needs to see final product too? -see if some-one will test it before final due date
4. Where will it be delivered? At Hamza's office					N/A
5. How will it be delivered? On Hamza's computer					-test it on a few computers before using Hamza's

A Moving Target

Even though the primary purpose of **The Accountability Tracking Tool** is to chart a UE's progress toward an agreed-upon benchmark, it can also be used by both the manager and the employee to monitor a range of other information. For example, Stephen found it very useful in keeping track of his thoughts, as well as his goal details. He created a version of the tool on his computer and PDA, and then created interim, weekly goals to help him reach his benchmark dates on time. He also used the tool as a place to note any questions he wanted to ask Julio, so that when they met, he had everything in one place.

Julio used **The Accountability Tracking Tool** as his working agenda for their weekly meetings. He and Stephen went over the tool each week to monitor progress and make joint updates. This gave them more of a sense of common purpose, and helped them to coordinate their efforts.

Result

Stephen and Julio already knew by early March that, although Stephen's program worked well for two users, there were problems when more than two sales managers tried to use it concurrently. Clearly, Stephen's next goal would be to solve this problem and regularly update Julio on his progress with a new tracking tool and new benchmarks. But instead of Julio having to remind Stephen about each of their new benchmark meetings, Stephen was now in the habit of periodic accountability. Technically, their trial run wasn't over—but Julio could already see that his accountability tracking system was working great!

As you can see, accountability metrics are never permanent targets. Your UE may agree to work toward certain benchmarks, but as the project he's working on, or goals he's trying to achieve, evolve, so will his accountability metrics. These changes are easy to manage with a little flexibility—just create a new set of benchmarks with your UE, and continue to work together. Even if you have to repeat this process often, you'll find that, over time, you become less engaged in setting accountability standards, because your UE will start to take more responsibility for his own performance.

Chapter 11 Summary

- *Accountability, or holding someone to their commitments, is vital to a UE salvage operation.*
- *In the beginning, you will be responsible for monitoring your UE's accountability. Eventually, the UE will learn to do it for himself.*
- *Ask these questions when tracking accountability:*
  - *What is being completed?*
  - *When will it be completed?*
  - *Who will it be delivered to?*
  - *Where will it be delivered?*
  - *How will it be delivered?*
- *Use* **The Accountability Tracking Tool** *to help you and your UE agree on benchmarks, and achieve them.*

Hot Tips	
If your UE says...	Try responding with...
"What's wrong with my performance?"	"On a scale of 1 to 10, with 10 being the highest, how do you think your overall performance rates?"
"Everything is getting done, so I don't understand your problem."	"Let's double-check that everything is getting done by going through your goals and milestones one by one. If there is a problem, I want to help you overcome any obstacles in your way."

Hot Tips	
If your UE says...	Try responding with...
"Don't you trust me to do what I say?"	"This isn't personal. This is about meeting your deadlines on time, so the team can move ahead. What's your status update?"
"Aren't you getting a little compulsive here?"	"Maybe I am, so help me out here. Which of your goals is a challenge for you right now?"
"It's insulting for you to check up on my every move."	"That's not my intent. My intent is to manage all the moving pieces on our team. What's the best way to do that with your pieces?"
"What's the difference if something is a little late?"	"We have tight deadlines. What would the impact be if everyone on our team was late with their deliverables?"
"Has it ever occurred to you that you have inflated expectations?"	"Maybe. Let's start from scratch and compare. What are your expectations for this project (goal)?

12

The Rude-nik

As you saw in **Chapter 11,** tracking tangible deliverables such as sales revenue, headcount, or an annual event is fairly straightforward with **The Accountability Tracking Tool.** (The important thing is that you set up your milestones and stick with tracking them!) But how do you track a "soft skill," or another deliverable intangible? How do you keep your UE accountable for a change in her mindset, or her attitude, or even for a behavior like rudeness? Will **The Accountability Tracking Tool** work for these kinds of deliverables as well?

The answer is *yes.*

Meet the Rude-nik

Being uncivil to a colleague, communicating in a hostile way, and backstabbing are all considered rude behaviors at work. Other behaviors that fit into this category include belittling a coworker's opinion, giving someone the cold shoulder, insulting a teammate's work, and interrupting someone in a condescending manner. Your UE may not display all of these traits, but you can be sure that even one of them negatively impacts your team's functioning, and therefore your organization's bottom line.

Case Study: Yolanda Takes It Too Far

At first, when his employee Yolanda went from being "assertive" to being downright rude, Bob tried to convince himself that either she was having a bout of artistic temperament or he was reacting to a generational difference, because Yolanda was much younger than Bob. But after Yolanda called one colleague a "little twerp," told another she was "useless and stupid," repeatedly interrupted a third, and told Bob to get out of her face—all in one week!—he was done kidding himself.

Problem

As the manager of a small marketing strategy company, Bob supervised many artistic employees, and he enjoyed the creativity of his diverse team. Yet Yolanda, his senior graphic designer, could no longer be excused for her behavior, for any reason. She wasn't being "Gen Y" *or* artistic; she was just plain unacceptably rude. Either Yolanda or her rudeness had to go!

Generations at Work

The presence of four generations at work—along with today's unprecedented multiculturalism—can greatly complicate the already difficult job of deciding where to draw the line with a UE. If Yolanda had been a Baby Boomer like Bob, he would have had a generational and a management model to deal with her firmly and confidently. But because she was two generations younger, he didn't know the best approach for handling her challenging behavior. You'll learn more about resolving generational problems like these in **Appendix A**.

193

Assessing an Employee's Worth

As much as he disliked her current behavior, Bob could easily recall several times when Yolanda's formerly positive assertiveness had been an asset to the team. Eight months before, she had fought for his backing to push the artistic boundaries on a client's Web design. Although it was difficult to convince the client, he'd ultimately been thrilled with Yolanda's work—and the Website had won a coveted design industry award. If Yolanda hadn't stood up for her vision, that site would never have seen the light of day.

And just six months before, she'd gone toe-to-toe with Bob over who to hire next for the team. Bob had wanted to bring another graphic artist onto the team, but Yolanda had argued (and persuaded him) that they really needed more copywriters. Bob had to admit it was one of the smartest moves they could have made.

Looking back on Yolanda's long track record, Bob couldn't help but feel that, in spite of her more recent behavior, he wasn't willing to let her go. On the other hand, he knew that recapturing Yolanda's value to the team was going to be a tall order, because her rudeness had caused serious ripples. To salvage this UE, Bob would have to deal with both Yolanda *and* the team members whose feelings (and pride) she'd managed to trample.

After deciding to commit to Yolanda, Bob undertook a series of low-key coaching conversations with members of his team. He was careful to keep these casual, and to hold them in places (and ways) that he believed would minimize the possibility of gossip. Among the questions he asked people were:

- *What are you noticing about Yolanda's current behavior?*
- *What's the impact of that behavior on you?*
- *What are her unique skills and strengths?*
- *Where does she contribute value to the team?*

The results of this thoroughly unscientific suvey were very encouraging to Bob. Although several people were quite angry, they all seemed willing to give Yolanda another chance—*if and when* she stopped her rude behavior. Armed with that knowledge, Bob began his salvage campaign.

Step...by Step...by Step...by Step

Over the next few months, Bob calculated that he was spending about 10 percent of his time on Yolanda, as he:

» *Completed* **The "What's It Worth?" Worksheet** *before committing to her retention* (**Step 1**).

» **Communicated** *with Yolanda about the need for her to stop her rude behavior* (**Step 2**).

» **Clarified** *her role on the team, and the team's goals* (**Step 3**).

» **Coached** *Yolanda, asking questions that he hoped would cause her to reflect on whether her recent behavior was helping her achieve her real objectives* (**Step 4**).

Some of these were one-time actions. Others were complex, requiring several conversations, or further strategizing on his part. In **Step 2**, for example, Bob and Yolanda discussed some of the ways she would need to change, but they also met with their HR manager and reviewed the company's Standard Operating Procedures (which were clear about the need to treat colleagues with respect) and the company's policies for disciplining employees who failed to meet the required behaviors (which included placing written reports in the employee's file).

In **Step 4**, to help Yolanda examine the impact of her behavior, Bob asked her the kind of open-ended, advice-free, and short coaching questions you learned about in **Chapter 10**, including:

» *What's the impact of your behavior on the team?*

» *What's the difference between assertive and aggressive?*

» *How do you want to behave with this team from now on?*

Finally, Bob felt confident that Yolanda knew there was a problem, had agreed to work on it, and had the information she needed to change her behavior. For **Step 5** of **The 5 Cs**, he was ready to use **The Accountability Tracking Tool** to ensure that she treated people appropriately moving forward.

195

Solution

As you remember from **Chapter 11, The Accountability Tracking Tool** is a simple chart that puts your expectations in writing, gives an overview of check-ins and deliverables, and keeps both you and your UE accountable for commitments. It does this by letting you answer these questions:

» *What is being completed?*
» *When will it be completed?*
» *Who will it be delivered to?*
» *Where will it be delivered?*
» *How will it be delivered?*

The Accountability Tracking Tool (Fill out for each agreed-upon deliverable.)					
Deliverable	Check-ins				Comments
What is being completed?					
When will it be completed?					
Who will it be delivered to?					
Where will it be delivered?					
How will it be delivered?					

Here is how the conversation about the tool started:

Bob: *Yolanda, I wanted to follow up on yesterday's meetings about the accepted behaviors for our team, which you agreed to abide by. In the past, your persistence was one of your best qualities. You rarely gave up on an idea that you thought was good for the team. I hope you apply the same persistence to changing your behavior over time, which isn't easy to do.*

Yolanda: *I can do anything I put my mind to. I don't need your help, or anyone else's. But I do need to know how you plan to measure and define "respect."*

Bob: *That's a good question, especially since there is no definition in the organizations SOPs. We're going to have to define it ourselves, with help from the other people on this team.*

Make-Your-Own Metrics

It's not uncommon to have a situation occur that is not in the SOPs or that HR has not clearly defined. So how does a manager handle that? With a little help from his friends. In this case, Bob needs to involve the whole team, so that everyone agrees on what respect means to their particular group. The steps he could take include:

1. *Meet with the entire team to open a conversation about "respect."*
2. *Get everyone's feedback on the workable definition of the term.*
3. *Create a final definition of "respect."*
4. *Describe the behaviors that show "respect."*

Each of these four steps is vital to success. If Bob doesn't involve the entire team in the conversation, he may miss important feedback and neglect to get buy-in from each team member. The team also needs to define "respect" together because everyone has different ideas about what this quality looks like in action. Depending on who's in the group, they might feel that you show respect by:

- *Not interrupting someone who's talking.*
- *Giving honest and timely feedback, even if you have to interrupt.*
- *Holding doors open for women.*
- *Allowing women to open doors for themselves.*
- *Addressing managers with their titles.*
- *Addressing managers by their first names.*

Any of these could be the correct behaviors and attitudes for one organization, but that doesn't mean that they're right for yours. And until you've defined *your own team's* standards, down to the specific behaviors, you can't hold people accountable for acting in specific ways.

So how do you define behavior? Behaviors are more than the things you do while working with your colleagues, clients, direct reports, and superiors. They include things such as how you dress, speak, argue your point, hold meetings, have a conversation, and more. Behaviors are where the "rubber" of attitude meets the "road" of relationships, to create an environment that lets people succeed.

Putting It Into Action

Bob began developing a metric for Yolanda by calling an informal team meeting to discuss how they could show respect for each other. Everyone was a little surprised, as this was not Bob's normal meeting style, but they all jumped into the conversation when he asked what the word *respect* meant to them. Bob wrote down all the ideas on a whiteboard, allowing everyone to give their feedback. It proved to be a lively and provocative meeting—and although no one agreed on the definition, they did have a few key words in common.

Bob then called a second meeting, where everyone brought in their own definitions. Though not everyone agreed 100 percent on what *respect* meant, they all agreed on the general intent. The team was able to reach consensus that *showing respect* would include these behaviors:

- *Don't interrupt others while they're speaking.*
- *Don't speak over other people in a side conversation.*

- *Fully focus in meetings: Turn off all phones, PDAs, and so forth.*
- *If you disagree with somone, make your point without raising your voice.*
- *Refrain from any threatening gestures.*
- *Avoid all profanity and derogatory words that are based on race, gender, or sexuality.*

This definition and the matching behaviors were then documented, with copies given to everyone on the team. It was also added to the departmental SOPs by HR, to be used for new employees in the small firm and to add to the disciplinary procedures.

Now that Bob and his team had clearly defined respect, it would be easier to track Yolanda's behavior change, using that definition as her "deliverable." When Bob and Yolanda completed **The Accountability Tracking Tool**, it looked like this:

The Accountability Tracking Tool (Fill out for each agreed-upon deliverable.)					
Deliverable	Check-ins				Comments
What is being completed? Respectful behavior toward everyone on team	5/7	5/14	5/28	6/8	Use the behaviors defined by the team
When will it be completed? Weekly milestone check-ins					
Who will it be delivered to? Everyone on team					

The Accountability Tracking Tool (Fill out for each agreed-upon deliverable.)					
Deliverable	Check-ins				Comments
Where will it be delivered? In office, on phone, by e-mail, in cafeteria—anywhere at work					
How will it be delivered? Verbally, nonverbally, and in writing					All behaviors will be evaluated

Yolanda and Bob conducted the weekly check-ins. Having a defined target helped both of them measure Yolanda's progress. If she felt that she was being respectful and Bob disagreed, they reviewed the agreed-upon behaviors to check. There was no guess work, and Bob did not have to shout to make his point; he could calmly refer to the behaviors defined by the team.

The Role of Responsibility

One of the benefits that became clear as Yolanda brought her rudeness under better control was the increased respect *she* enjoyed on the team. Many UEs don't understand that taking responsibility for their actions is not just their key to success on the job; it's also key to how much influence, even power, they're given by others on their team.

People who take responsibility generally inspire confidence in others, and are granted influence because of it. But people who shirk responsibility, play the victim, and blame others for their failures are marginalized and have little influence. If a UE is operating in victim mode, his colleagues won't want to work with him, and his manager will hesitate to assign anything important to him. He'll have very little influence on the team, largely as a result of his own decision to avoid responsibility.

On the other hand, as Yolanda discovered, as a UE begins to take responsibility for all aspects of his behavior, his colleagues will begin to trust him more. Assuming that he's good at his job, they'll listen more closely to what he has to say. His influence will gradually increase—again, as a result of his own actions—which will motivate him to take more responsibility. Anything that you can do to encourage the start of this virtuous cycle will benefit everyone involved: your team, your UE, and yourself.

What to Do When Your UE Backtracks

One month later, Yolanda had a serious setback. One of her coworker Marie's clients was being even more demanding than usual, at a time when many other deadlines were due and everyone was working long hours. Everyone was feeling hassled, and fuses were getting short. In a meeting where Marie was (once again!) attempting to outline a solution for her client's latest complaint to the team, Yolanda snapped.

"That's the stupidest &^% idea I ever heard of,"* she yelled. *"Where did you come up with that stinker?"*

Bob immediately stood up and asked Yolanda to step outside with him. He could have waited until the meeting was over to respond to her actions, but he didn't want to risk another outbreak of temper during the meeting. He also wanted to show the rest of his team that he'd truly instituted a zero-tolerance policy for rudeness. When he and Yolanda had left the room, they had the following conversation:

Bob: *Yolanda, you cursed and raised your voice to Marie, which is against our definition of respect. What caused that?*

Yolanda: *I know, I know. It just slipped out. I was tired, hungry, frustrated, and sick of hearing about this client. I get snarky when I'm feeling stressed like that. I'm sorry.*

Bob: *I appreciate that, and am also going to ask you to apologize to Marie directly. And then we'll have to have HR handle this.*

As you know, after the meeting we held two months ago, our HR policy states that the first violation the first violation gets written up.

Yolanda: *I know.*

Bob: *You've made great progress in the past three months, and I'll note that in the write-up. You slipped today, but I'm confident that you can move forward from this mistake. I've seen you do it before, and I know I'll see you do it again. If not, then you know HR's the next step, right?*

Yolanda: *Yes. And I'm not going to let a second warning get into my file.*

Bob: *I believe you! Remember, if someone else is getting on your nerves, come talk to me before you feel like you're going to explode.*

Yolanda: *Okay. I'll try to do that.*

After that incident, Yolanda had no more backslides. Bob kept her tightly accountable, and continued to use the team's definition of respect as the metric for her behavior. They both understood the implications for her future, and Bob was particularly gratified by the climate of *respect* that now characterized his team.

As you can see, it's possible to track tangible goals, as well as intangible goals, by defining the behaviors that comprise the goal. Once behavioral parameters are decided, **The Accountability Tracking Tool** will help you help your UE move from unmanageable back to valuable.

Chapter 12 Summary

- *Accountability is just as important for intangible as for tangible goals.*
- *When creating metrics for an intangible goal that is not in your SOPs, be sure to get input, feedback, and buy-in from every member of your team.*
- *In addition to defining the goal with words, be sure to describe it behaviorally. Knowing how "respect" or "responsibility" look in action makes it possible to observe and assess how well your UE is meeting those goals.*

◇◇

» *Once behavioral benchmarks are set, use* **The Accountability Tracking Tool** *to monitor your UE's actions.*

Hot Tips	
If your UE says...	Try responding with...
"You got a problem with how I talk?"	"I value respectful communication. What does respectful communication sound like to you?"
"People piss me off; so what?"	"It's important to manage emotions at work so that they don't interrupt the whole team. How can you manage your emotions without negatively impacting the team?"
"I guess you've been spying on me, haven't you!"	"What makes you think that?"
"Why don't you ever crack on other people when they do something rude?"	"I try to be fair with the team. If I'm not, please give me specific details. In the meantime, let's get back to your behavior."
"You think everybody treats me so perfectly?"	"How would you like to be treated at work?"
"What are you gonna do about it, huh?"	"If you were in my shoes, what would you do in this situation?"
"What's in it for me to act better? You don't like me anyway."	"This isn't about personalities. It's about team performance. How would changing your behavior benefit you?"

13

When It's Time to Call It Quits

In **Chapter 3**, you saw how the **"What's it Worth?" Worksheet** will help you evaluate the true cost of your UE's unmanageable behavior. Armed with this information, you can determine whether the benefits of UE salvage are worth the time and effort they'll require. If the answer is yes, **The 5 Cs** will guide you to the best possible outcome—hopefully, a complete turnaround of your unmanageable's behavior.

But what if the answer is no? What if it's just not worth trying to salvage this particular UE? What if your unmanageable has either not established her value, or has already cost you more than her potential is worth? In that case, **The "What's it Worth?" Worksheet** provides a way to objectively confirm what you may have already suspected: that you're not going to invest more time, energy, and money in this unmanageable situation. When that happens—when your answer to the question *"What's it worth?"* is *"Not enough!"*—it's time to call it quits.

Meet The AWOL

Though the military definition of AWOL—absent without leave—implies desertion, the phrase carries a less formal definition in the business world. In business, someone who's AWOL might be late, or a no-show; might have disappeared for days, or wandered off after lunch; or might be physically present but mentally absent, neglecting his duties. When someone goes AWOL, her work piles up, deadlines are missed, and projects don't move forward. And having an AWOL on your team creates a constant, low-grade sense of anxiety, as you and your team members hustle to figure out (once again!) who'll cover for her.

Case Study: Better Late Than Never? Not Isaac!

Isaac was never there when Priti needed him. He was consistently late for work, late for meetings, and late to return important phone calls. Some days, he didn't show up at all. Although Priti had hired him with high hopes, it was clear that she couldn't count on him to take on any significant tasks, because she never knew when he'd go AWOL.

Problem

Priti wore many hats at her small start-up company. Her official title was CEO, but because she had limited VC funding, she was also the CFO, the marketing manager, and everything else.

That's why she was so thrilled when Isaac—a four-year college marketing graduate she'd met when he interned at her previous job—agreed to come onboard as the company's sales receptionist. He was overqualified for the position, but that was the kind of help she needed right then, and they both agreed that, as the company grew, he would move into marketing.

Because of Priti's hopes for the future (and because of his previously solid record), she chose to ignore the first signs that Isaac was becoming a UE. The first time Isaac was late for work, he had a valid explanation. The following week, he was late twice more—but only for 10 minutes each time. One day, he didn't show up for work at all. He later told Priti that he hadn't realized he was supposed to call in if he was sick. (Yes, Priti acknowledged to Isaac, it was true that her start-up hadn't defined any SOPs, but she couldn't help thinking that a 10-year-old would know to call in if he was sick!)

But then came an incident she couldn't ignore: Craig Whitmore, one of Priti's biggest clients, had called to request that his $3,000 product contract be finalized within 24 hours. His message said that he was in a mad rush, and that if Priti couldn't deliver, he'd have to find someone else who could. Isaac was 15 minutes late for work that day, which is why Whitmore's message went into voice mail. Still, things would have worked out fine except that Isaac never *checked* the voice mails. And Whitmore—whose bite was as bad as his bark—did give the contract to someone else.

If your employee is becoming unmanageable, he will eventually hit you with an action that you can't rationalize away. Even if you've ignored earlier trouble signs, turn to **The "What's it Worth?" Worksheet** at the first *undeniable* problem. Continuing to sidestep reality past this point is a guarantee that, by the time you decide to come to grips with your UE, things will have gotten much, much worse.

Dig In!

Some managers would rather have a root canal than complete a detailed **"What's it Worth?" Worksheet.** We know–it's not always a fun exercise. But take the time to do your number crunching before you make a decision. Whether your answer is thumbs up or down, you need to confirm that your decision is based on actual data and careful reasoning.

Solution

Here is how Priti's **"What's it Worth?" Worksheet** helped her reach a decision about Isaac (see **Chapter 3** for a more detailed explanation of how to complete the worksheet):

Part 1: Cost of the UE's Problem

When Priti calculated her own time, she was upset to discover how much she'd invested and how out of hand she'd let things get with Isaac. Because she was working a 60-hour week at her start-up salary of $50,000, the annual cost of *just her time* to manage him would be $2,500!

Estimated Cost of Manager's Time	Hrs./Week	6 Mo. Cost
Time spent with UE	1.5 hrs./wk.	--
Time spent with other involved employees	.5 hr./wk.	--
Time with HR, lawyer, or senior management	1 hr./wk.	--
Time managing fallout with clients	-	--
Other	--	--
Total Estimated Cost of Manager's Time	3 hrs./wk.	$1,250

Tick Tock

Time adds up, little by little. If you're not a detail-oriented person, carry a notebook or your PDA to track what you're doing during every 10–15 minute slot. You'll probably be surprised, when you take careful note of your week's activities, to learn how much time is getting eaten up by UE management.

Priti calculated the cost of lost employee productivity as follows:

Estimated Cost of Lost Employee Productivity	Percentage	6 Mo. Cost
Productivity lost by the UE	5%	$625
Productivity lost by other involved employees	5%	$750
Other	--	--
Total Estimated Cost of Lost Employee Productivity	--	~$1,375

She then recorded the lost Whitmore contract as an "other" direct UE cost (grinding her teeth as she wrote down the number).

Estimated Direct Costs	Current	6 Mos. Cost
Compensation for product or service mistakes	--	--
Costs of damage to equipment, etc.	--	--
Other	$3,000	--
Total Estimated Direct Costs	$3,000	--

As far as UE opportunity costs, Priti realized that, because of time spent working with or worrying about Isaac, she had neglected to create key relationships with partners who could distribute her product. Those relationships were potentially worth $200,000 to her start-up in the next year, because getting her product out the door was her number one challenge. Put in those terms, Priti could see that, over six months, Isaac would cost her somewhere between $5,600 over six months, and the future of her entire company.

◇◇

When It's Time to Call It Quits

Although opportunity costs can be hard to calculate, they are critically important. The reality is that, if you're always putting out fires, you won't have time to develop the opportunities that may take your organization to the next level; and an organization that doesn't grow is at greater and greater risk of failing.

Estimated Opportunity Costs	Current	6 Mo. Cost
Missed deadlines	--	--
Bids not completed	--	--
Projects not developed	--	$200,000
Other	--	--
Total Estimated Opportunity Costs	--	$200,000

Part 2: Estimated Cost of "UE Salvage Operation"

As you've learned, UE salvage *always* takes time, money, and focus that could be devoted to other things. And conversely, as we discussed in **Chapter 3**, the cost of replacing any employee is high—starting at 30 to 50 percent of annual salary for entry-level workers, and rising as high as 400 percent of salary for people with specialized, high-level skills. Although that was an argument for keeping Isaac, Priti found that it didn't sway her numbers or reasoning. His attitude and performance weren't improving at all, so it was hard to imagine giving him even more time, energy, or attention. Even the two hours per week she grudgingly allocated on **The "What's it Worth?" Worksheet** was too much:

Estimated Cost of "UE Salvage Operation"	Hrs./Week	6 Mo. Cost
Manager's time	2	~$800

Internal consultant's time (HR, legal, etc.)		
External consultant evaluation (if desired)		
External coaching (for UE and/or manager)		
Other		
Total Estimated Cost of "UE Salvage Operation"	2	~$800
Estimated Cost of UE Replacement (2–2.5 x annual salary)	$50,000	

Part 3: Benefits of "UE Salvage"

Priti's inclinations were reinforced when she filled out this section:

Benefits of "UE Salvage"
Was your UE ever a fully productive employee? If so, what was his/her major contribution? Not at the current job. However, he was great as an intern at my previous corporate job. Maybe the start-up situation isn't best for him?
What would this UE contribute to your team if he/she was functioning fully now? After learning about the company as our receptionist, he might be a good marketing manager.
What incremental benefits from his/her participation might be captured over time? It's hard to even answer this, because I can't rely on him anymore.

◇◇

When It's Time to Call It Quits

It was now completely clear to Priti that the expectations she'd had for Isaac were based on the past, not his present performance; that the $5,600+ he would cost over six months was a ridiculous use of her money; and that she needed qualified professional staff, not an unreliable trainee.

Facing the fact that she had made a poor hiring choice, Priti gave Isaac his notice and started looking for a new receptionist. This took her about a month, but after onboarding her new employee, Priti knew she'd made the right decision. She no longer worried about lateness, no-shows, and missed messages. And she was—finally!—able to focus on growing her company through the distribution channels that she was cultivating.

If, like Priti, you decide to let your UE go *before* trying a salvage operation, you may also experience these rapid benefits. But sometimes managers commit to UE salvage and later change their minds because their UE just doesn't respond (or worse, deteriorates). This happened to one of Anne's clients, Lorena, who was a VP in a multinational organization:

> *After completing the cost-benefit analysis, Lorena committed to a salvage operation for her UE Cliff, an Excuse-Maker. Together, Cliff and Lorena worked through* **The 5 Cs**, *agreeing to the problem and clarifying the roles. Lorena became a skilled coach and held Cliff tightly accountable for his goals. Yet, in spite of their combined efforts, Cliff didn't change his behavior. He still blamed everyone else for his own missed deadlines, refused to accept his role in any conflict, and continued to act irritably toward many of his colleagues. Lorena hated to let Cliff go, because he was highly skilled in his area of expertise, but she could no longer tolerate behavior that was dragging down her entire team.*

Planning for Goodbye

When you're ready to let an employee go, it's important to proceed with the same discipline and transparency that you've used while working through **The 5 Cs.** Before choosing a course of action, become thoroughly familiar with your company's rules, regulations, and expectations regarding the process of firing someone. Your organization's culture, legal guidelines, and standard HR procedures should be given priority over anything in this book. If you are unclear about your company's policies and procedures, confer with HR or your appropriate higher-ups.

That said, here are some general guidelines and tips that you should keep in mind:

- **Set a time limit and stick to it.** *UE problems almost never resolve themselves, so don't ignore your UE's behavior in the hope that it will magically go away. If your UE has not significantly improved after six months of* **5 Cs** *intervention (the average amount of time it takes to see sustained behavioral change), it's probably time for you to cut your losses and move on.*
- **Give clear, honest, open, and, most of all, constant feedback regarding the problem to the UE.** *Your first conversation about dismissal must not be the one in which your UE gets fired. This is ground that must be carefully prepared—in discussions of dismissal as a possible consequence for unmanageable behavior, in reviews of your organization's policies, and, preferably, in written reports or evaluations that your UE has had a chance to examine. Firing is not a first resort, and should never come as a surprise to your employee.*
- **Document and report everything to the appropriate people.** *At the first hint that you may want to dismiss your UE, begin to keep a detailed and regular log of all relevant facts, dates, and incidents. Records of your UE's behavior should be specific ("He yelled at John, calling him incompetent, during 1/19 staff meeting" rather than "He has a bad attitude toward his teammates.") Carefully record the steps you've taken to address and correct the problem, including conversations with the UE, consults with HR or others, coaching sessions, write-ups, and so*

forth. Keep this log and a backup copy in a safe and private location, so that, if you are called on to legally defend your decision, you can provide clear documentation of the legitimate business reasons that led to dismissal. Again consult your HR manual and talk to your higher-ups for advice and guidance, particularly if you have never before had to fire an employee.

- **Make a plan, and work it.** *In tandem with HR and your own higher-ups, create a plan for this situation, and get everyone's buy-in on that plan. Do not wing it, and do not take sole responsibility for either how your UE is fired, or for what will happen after she goes. Areas that should be discussed and agreed upon in advance, with your boss and/or HR, include who will perform your UE's duties; where, how, and when will you start looking for a replacement; and how and by whom will your new employee be trained. Be sure that you also understand how your UE's employment references will be handled. Consult your legal/HR manuals for guidance on this, as you may have a legal obligation to disclose truthful, if negative, information to prospective employers.*
- **Don't ignore your other employees.** *Give your non-UE employees as much time, focus, and attention as you can, throughout this entire situation. All parents know that a "problem child" can easily gobble up their time and attention, leaving other children to fend for themselves, and potentially turning them unmanageable. Hard as it is to juggle everyone, don't let this happen in your department!*

Tips for the Dismissal

- **Get to the point quickly and make it brief.** *Don't beat around the bush or try and soften the blow by speaking euphemistically. Tell the truth, in a direct* *and respectful manner. Don't "tell it slant"—in other words, don't put a bright face or a PR spin on things.*

- **Be empathetic.** *Don't fire the employee in front of other people. Avoid speaking harshly or shaming him. Remember that you are dealing with a human being who has an ego, possibly a family, perhaps a mortgage, bills to pay, or medical needs. Empathy does not mean trying to solve his problems—don't ask how he's going to get by, for instance—but it does mean speaking with respect, even kindness. Keeping the humanity of your UE in mind will help both of you get through this experience.*
- **Expect and plan for a bad reaction.** *Your UE could become emotional, expressing rage, grief, or anxiety. Listen calmly, but be firm. Don't let your encounter devolve into a "he said-she said" situation. Stay on topic and remind the UE of all the previous conversations and write-ups by saying "Due to all the reasons we've discussed, this is the decision that's been made."*
- **Do not forget safety considerations, particularly if you're dealing with someone who seems strange, threatening, irrational, or emotionally unstable in any other way.** *Look at past behavior and attend to your instincts, as well as those of others. Have any other employees come to you expressing fear or discomfort around this person? Have you ever seen your UE behave in a threatening or irrational way? If so, make sure you're not the only person standing between your former UE and her job (or the front door). Ask your HR or higher-ups in advance for assistance with security if you have any concerns about how this person will react at the time of dismissal.*
- **Make it final.** *Your UE should be clear that this is the last time she will be on the premises. Arrange for security to escort her out, if you feel that may be necessary.*

Your UE has been a huge drain on your energy and your organization's resources, and you probably expect that, when she's gone, you'll be (at least figuratively) dancing for joy. But don't be surprised if your thoughts and feelings after the fact are not as clear or straightforward as you expected. That's because, for most people, firing someone is a very big deal—no matter how responsibly you act or how deserved the firing was. A day or two of stress is only natural, but if you continue to feel guilty or upset about the firing, ask your boss or an appropriate HR representative for help, advice, or backup so that you can focus on taking care of *yourself*. Don't forget to remind yourself that you did everything possible to help this person. And take some time to explain your decision to your other employees. Most importantly, let your team know that your door is open if anyone needs to talk about what happened.

Chapter 13 Summary

- *Even if you've ignored other warning signs, make the earliest possible decision to* **Commit or Quit.**
- *Use* **The "What's it Worth?" Worksheet** *to reach your decision and to make sure it's grounded in objective reality.*
- *If it's time to let your UE go, do so with respect, compassion, and dignity, no matter how unmanageable the employee was.*
- *Plan carefully, and be sure to consult with your HR liaison or higher-ups before starting the dismissal process.*
- *Do not make yourself the bad guy in a dismissal. Make sure that it's clear this was an organizational decision.*
- *Don't be surprised if you need a little recovery time after this stressful experience. Take care of yourself, as well as your team members.*

Conclusion

Congratulations on the journey you've just taken! We hope it's been an exciting one, and that, as you reach the finish line, you're confident about you new abilities to manage your unmanagable and motivate your team.

Your guide to that process will be **The 5 Cs**—and as you now know, each of its steps are foundational, with Step 1 laying the foundation for Step 2, Step 2 laying the foundation for Step 3, and so on. Depending on your particular UE, you may not need to spend equal, or even lengthy, amounts of time on each step, but be sure that you touch on each of them:

1. *Commit or Quit*
2. *Communicate*
3. *Clarify Goals and Roles*
4. *Coach*
5. *Create Accountability*

You've also learned that no two UEs are alike. Although we've given you composites of the most common UEs we've encountered, your unmanageable will likely look different—perhaps in very unique and challenging ways. *Does this mean your UE can't be salvaged?* Not at all! It's just a reminder that people are different, and there's no cookie-cutter approach to working with human beings. So let **The 5 Cs** guide you, and give you a flexible structure to count on, as you work with your UE. Knowing that you have this framework will give you confidence, inspire your creativity, and even help you relax a little!

And relaxing about your UE is a good thing. Think about it: How often does your unmanageable drive you insane, or cause your blood pressure to rise? You've probably lost count by now, but you can be assured that your UE (and everyone else that you work with) sees you stressing, feels your tension, and worries about you and the team. The more you're able to relax—and what's more relaxing than having a plan!—the easier your UE salvage operation will be.

Appendix A
How to Manage Three Generations

From blog posts by Anne Loehr, dubbed the "Generational Guru" by *The Washington Post*

The "Good Old Days"

It used to be that people entered the work force after school and climbed slowly, steadily up the ladder to retirement.

But in today's rapidly changing world, *wunderkind* run companies and grandparents take entry-level jobs. If you walk into a conference room and see a 30-year-old, a 45-year-old, and a 60-year-old sitting at the table, don't assume you know who's the boss; it could be any of them. And this can create "unmanageable" situations for everyone involved.

Today's managers face the formidable task of supervising *three* generations at once, with age groups mixing at virtually every level. Where once there were rules for how to treat people of other generations, now it sometimes seems as if it's "every manager for herself."

And yet, to effectively leverage the strengths of each generation in today's workplace, you need to understand how to manage them. That means knowing at least something about the core beliefs and values, history, traits, and culture of each generation.

In this appendix, we are going to look at:

» *A quick overview of three generational groups in today's workforce.*
» *The differences and similarities of each generation.*
» *The language to use with each generation.*
» *How each generation prefers to interact.*
» *How to delegate effectively to each generation.*

Here's a quick overview of the three predominant generational groups in today's workplace. Although some Traditionalists (people from the generation before Baby Boomers, sometimes called "The Greatest Generation") may still be in the workforce, we are going to focus on the other three generations.

Baby Boomers

Born 1946–1964

Baby Boomers still embrace the values of "the 1960s" (which, in fact, stretched well into the mid-1970s). They are rebels who will happily break the rules for a good cause (or even just because they feel like it).

In general, Baby Boomers were shaped by Vietnam and Civil Rights, the women's movement, and the successful American effort to place the first man on the moon. From these dramatic events, Boomers collaborated as a whole so their voices could be heard and changes made. Consequently, Boomers tend to be idealistic, ambitious, optimistic, consensus-driven, and cause-driven. They value community and political correctness, and they want their work to have meaning.

Boomers were also the first American generation to be exalted (and fiercely courted) by marketers for their youth. Evidence to the contrary, most Baby Boomers still believe that they are young, and still believe they are at the center of all things.

Generation X

Born 1965–1980

Generation X children, whose parents were likely young Baby Boomers, often had to fend for themselves. So it's not surprising that this generation has a self-sufficient approach to life.

The "Me Generation" works hard, plays hard, and takes success very seriously. Gen X experienced the aftermath of Watergate, the explosion of the shuttle *Challenger*, skyrocketing divorce rates (their parents and their own), and the launch of MTV. These events reinforced their belief that neither families nor governments would look after them—and made them even more pragmatic, results-driven, work-focused, and materialistic.

Although many Boomers feel "sandwiched" between the needs of aging parents and growing children, it could be argued that Generation X managers—caught between the demands of independent, soon-to-be-retiring Baby Boomer executives and communal Gen Y employees—are the true "sandwich generation."

Generation Y

Born 1981–2001

The first truly high-tech generation, also known as the "Millennials" or "Digital Natives," is tolerant and diverse. Having grown up with unlimited access to information, many of Generation Y's members are highly educated and authentically self-confident.

Because Gen Y was wired from day one, they expect everything to be "downloaded" immediately. Any global event is online in seconds, so studies show that a 10-year-old Gen Y has the maturity level of a 16-year-old Boomer. They are as diverse as the globe, and value connections, wanting to be part of a community at home, work, and play. They had a voice at "family meetings," so have the confidence to articulate, the tech skills to create, and the community to support them in their vision of success.

◇◇

Appendix A

Like their Baby Boomer parents (or grandparents), Gen Ys are intensely focused on social, political, and ecological issues. A large generation, they have the desire to create positive change—and they might just have the confidence and talent to succeed!

Generational Nuances

Now that you understand these points, it's time to look at some of the personal nuances that can influence your generational identity.

Family Nuances

Birth order can have an influence on a generational personality. For example, I was born in 1965, in the first year of Gen X. So technically speaking, I'm a "cusper" (meaning, born on the cusp). However, because I'm the youngest of eight children—and followed my older siblings around the house, listened to their music, and tried to act like them—I have Baby Boomer tendencies. On the other hand, if I had been the *oldest* of eight children (while still being born in 1965), I would be much more of a Gen X-er, because my siblings would have learned their generational culture from me. But since that didn't happen, I have more Boomer tendencies than Gen X tendencies, even though I'm in the Gen X demographic.

International Nuances

Living overseas also influences a generational personality. In general, living overseas during the formative teen years—even for a short period of time—tends to mature a child. So if someone has lived overseas, he or she tends to bump up to the previous generation. For example, my husband was born in 1967, so he is definitely in the Gen X category. However, he grew up in Kenya, Africa. Growing up in a foreign culture demanded more maturity from him, so, although he definitely has a Gen X style, he has far more Boomer tendencies than his compatriots who were raised in the United States.

Military Nuances

Growing up in the military also influences your generational personality. Not only do children of military employees often live overseas, they also tend to be influenced by the military itself, which tends to be more traditional than mainstream America. So if someone is the child of a military employee, he or she also tends to bump up to the previous generation. For example, Sean was born in 1970, so he is a solid Gen X. However, he not only grew up in the military, he also went to West Point Academy. Therefore, he is an "X," with more Boomer traits than many of his Gen X friends.

Relocating to the United States

Many people tell me that they don't feel like the generation they were "born into." When we look into their formative years, it turns out that often they grew up overseas, moved to the United States for college, and later became U.S. citizens. Although they have lived in the United States for more years than they lived in their place of birth, they still lived overseas during their *formative* years, which bumps them up a generation. Eileen, an Irishwoman with an American accent, said *"I just don't get Gen X, and I'm supposed to be one of them! I relate much better to colleagues who are older than myself."* That's because Ireland is more traditional in many ways than the United States; this type of tradition matured her, and made her more like the older generation.

When Things Go Wrong Between Generations at Work

Imagine that three different cultures are trying to assimilate and adapt to each other, in real time. That's just what's going on in today's workplace, as independent Boomers, hard-driving Gen X, and sociable Gen Y learn to work together.

Often, these *ad hoc* efforts are successful. But when things go wrong between generations, they can sometimes go *very* wrong:

Mary, the Baby Boomer CEO of a large printing company, had been trying for days to reach Dan, her newly hired Gen X manager in L.A. She wanted him to fly to Washington, D.C. to meet with her and a big potential client, but Dan wasn't responding to her calls. Frustrated and angry, Mary met with the prospect alone. She couldn't believe that Dan had just ignored her request to attend a major meeting, and was starting to think about firing him.

Fortunately, Mary brought this story to me during our regular consultation. I noted that Baby Boomers and Gen X communicate differently, and asked Mary, "Do you know how to text?"

"No," *Mary replied.* "Why should I?" *In answer, I borrowed Mary's phone and discovered that she had* **12** *unread text messages from Dan. Far from ignoring her messages, Dan had used what he considered the quickest and most attention-getting way to respond, but Mary had no idea he'd been trying to reach her.*

Of course, technology is not the only source of communication problems between the generations. Sometimes, the very words we choose can show how far apart the generations are:

Tom, a 35-year-old manager, supervises a team of research scientists. He expects the best from each team member, and often gives them pep talks, saying, "I want each of you to shoot for your personal best. Be the high scorer on this team! Show me everything you've got." *Baby Boomer Grace has nothing against sports, but (like many of her peers) she isn't motivated by beating others. She would be far more excited if, just once, Tom would tell the team,* "If this entire team pulls together, I know we can do great things!" *But that language is foreign to Tom, and he doesn't understand the impact it would have on his Baby Boomer employees.*

Introducing the Three Generations

A growing body of research shows that the Baby Boomer, Gen X, and Gen Y generations have different priorities, personalities, language preferences, and values, shaped by the differing political, social, and technological events that occurred during each group's formative years.

Movie Star Generations

To picture the generations in action, film fans can think about the varied careers and personalities of Meryl Streep (a Baby Boomer), Angelina Jolie (Gen X), and Kirsten Dunst (Gen Y); or Robert DeNiro (Boomer), Matt Damon (Gen X), and Daniel Radcliffe (Gen Y).

This doesn't mean that every member of a generation is the same! But it *does* mean that, as you learn to manage your "unmanageable" employees, an eye to their generation will serve you well. It's a lens—one tool—that may help you break communication barriers. It's not the only management tool to use; however, it's a powerful one when used correctly.

And opportunities always abound:

- *The other day I heard a friend say,* "I can't work with them. They are the problem." *Was my friend discussing people from another office? People from another country? From another political party? No, she was talking about people from another generation—Gen Y!*
- *And later I overheard a similar discussion in an elevator, with one Gen Y saying to another,* "I can't wait for them to retire, so we can take over." *What was she discussing? Baby Boomers.*

The generational issue at work causes emotions to rise. It can also create polarity and discord. It's not as if Baby Boomers, Gen X, and Gen Y are from three different species; they're all creative, hard-working human beings. However, they also have different perspectives on life, based on the events that shaped and influenced their formative years.

If we could understand each generation's perspective, we could then start to understand the generations better, and eventually work with them more effectively. Once you learn what shaped each generation, it's easier to understand their perspective, and find ways to relate to and work with them.

I was discussing this in a group, and a Gen X colleague said, *"Gen Y saw a lot of changes in their life—like 9/11 and the Iraq war. No wonder they feel a need for constant communication and connection; life is precious to them."*

Another Boomer colleague added, *"If Gen Y grew up on reality TV, they think that's a normal way to talk and interact. They didn't have any strong role models for professional behavior."*

And a Gen Y colleague added, *"It must be hard to be a Boomer. There were so many of you. You really had to fight hard to get the job you wanted, or to even get noticed. But Gen X had it easy, as there were so few of them. They didn't have to worry so much about finding a job. That explains a lot about their behavior."*

As you can see, just starting the conversation about each generation opened the door to awareness and insights. If you want your organization to work smarter and more effectively, find 30 to 40 minutes for a generational talk. At the meeting, let everyone know about the three generations in the workforce, and what shaped them.

It won't make the problems go away, but it's a first step toward changing *them* to *we*.

How to Speak So Each Generation Will Listen

When you have the generational talk that I'm suggesting, understanding each generation's language will also help you build rapport and trust between the groups, and avoid problems that might become unmanageable.

Why is it so difficult for so many people? Because each generation has a distinctly separate view of work, life, and society. There is no right or wrong generational viewpoint. However, there is a right and wrong approach. Each generation must be approached using certain keywords, tailor-made to fit that generation's traits.

Imagine working in Japan, Argentina, Norway, and South Africa. In order to work effectively in each location, you would likely take the time to learn some of the language, habits, and history of each country. This better prepares you to work with each culture.

The same applies for the three main generations in today's workplace. You must be prepared to speak three languages and learn three sets of habits if you want to be effective with each generation. If you speak Japanese in Argentina, you will fail in effectively communicating with the Argentine. If you speak Gen Y to a Gen X employee, you will also fail in making your point with the employee.

Each of these generations was influenced by certain events that shaped their psyche during their formative years. The formative years tend to take place 10 to 20 years after a person was born, so let's look at the events that shaped each generation during their formative years.

Baby Boomers

Born between 1946 and 1964

(Formative years between approximately 1957 and 1974)

Three of the dominant events that shaped this generation were the assassinations of JKF, MLK, and Robert Kennedy; every Boomer remembers where they were when JFK was shot. (Do you? If not, you're likely Gen X or Gen Y!) The Vietnam War also had a huge impact on Boomers. From these dramatic events, they saw that they had to band together so their voices could be heard and changes could be made. They learned that they could indeed change the world if they collaborated as a whole.

Details are important to Boomers, because they saw that legislative details made the difference in stopping the Vietnam War and starting the civil rights movement. Man landing on the moon also impacted this generation; it showed them that anything was possible and the sky was literally the limit. On that momentous day, they learned that nothing was impossible for a Boomer!

Free love was a big influence during this era. This allowed Boomers to explore themselves, as well as the world; they are still a dominant force in the travel industry. Finally, they are also the first generation where a majority went to college and climbed up the corporate ladder; consequently they are time-stressed as they struggle to manage 60-hour work weeks.

As a result of these events, Boomers tend to be idealistic, politically correct, consensus-driven, and cause-driven. They also tend to break the rules and truly want to change the world for the better.

Now that you understand which events shaped this generation, and how Boomers view the world, how can you best connect with them? You use keywords and key phrases that resonate with them. When you do this, they then feel understood and are willing to listen to you. You build rapport, so they will engage with you more willingly. If you continue to use their keywords and key phrases, you will have an effective conversation with them, simply by using their own language.

Keywords and Key Phrases for Boomers:

- *Make a difference*
- *Consensus*
- *Team/we*
- *Save time*
- *Features and benefits*

So if you're trying to convince a Boomer to launch a new Website, you would say something like, "*The team feels that launching this Website will make a big difference to the success of our company. We've tried some new features; the BB widget will save our employees two hours/week. Imagine what would happen if we all had an extra two hours in our day. It's a win-win for everyone!*"

How to Speak So Gen X Will Listen

Born between 1965 and 1980

(Formative years between approximately 1976 and 1990)

Not only did Gen X face three recessions and stagflation during their formative years, but they also dealt with the aftermath of Watergate, the beginning of the Gulf War, and the unprecedented *Challenger* explosion. From these events, Gen X often felt that they couldn't trust their government to look after them.

In addition, Gen X saw divorce rates skyrocket. Latchkey kids, after-school daycare, and full-time working mothers became the norm.

What did Gen X take away from this? That they often couldn't trust their family to take care of them either.

During this time, they also saw career situations change. No longer were their Boomer relatives safe in a job for 30 years. All of a sudden, jobs were getting cut and career stability was eroding. Consequently, Gen X received MBA degrees in droves, so that they could be "safe" from all the workplace changes.

MTV also changed their world. This allowed them a place to escape to. It also gave Gen X access to celebrity lifestyles; being ostentatious was hip if it meant you could be a "Material Girl" like Madonna.

Gen X felt early on that they couldn't trust their government, the corporate world or their families do not discintegrate in front of their eyes. So they tend to be self-sufficient and pragmatic. They also tend to be distrustful of hierarchy, based on what they saw in their formative years; therefore they *must* know what's in it for them before they take any action. Finally, MTV taught them how to be individualistic and view material wealth differently than their parents.

Now that you understand which events shaped this generation, and how Gen X view the world, how can you best connect with them? You use keywords and key phrases that resonate with them. When you do this, they then feel understood and are willing to listen to you. You build rapport, so they will engage with you more willingly. If you continue to use their keywords and key phrases, you will have an effective conversation with them, simply by using their own language.

Keywords and Key Phrases for Gen X:

- *Best, finest, world-class*
- *Independent*
- *"You will benefit by..."*
- *Data/numbers*

So if you're trying to convince a Gen Xer to launch a new Website, you would say something like, *"This Website is going to be the best in the industry. You will be seen as the creative visionary who inspired the team to launch a new concept. I've done my research and the best way to go about it systematically is...."*

◇◇

Appendix A

As you can see, this is very different language than you would use with Baby Boomers. The message is still the same; you want the person to consider launching a website. Yet, the language has changed so that the Gen Xer can actually hear you. Have you sold the person on the idea? No, not yet. However, you have tapped into her language so that she is listening to you instead of tuning you out. That's the first step toward creating a relationship with Gen X.

How to Speak So Gen Y Will Listen

Born between 1981 and 2000

(Formative years between approximately 1992 and present)

Gen Y is also known as Millennials, Echo-Boomers, and the Net Generation. No matter what you call them, they are a powerful force of 79+ million (almost as big as the Baby Boomer generation). They were wired from day one; consequently, they are called Digital Natives, whereas the other generations are known as Digital Immigrants. This generation was born with a mouse in its hand and studies are showing that, as a result, they process information differently than the other generations. What does this mean? Not only are they tech-savvy, they also expect everything to be "downloaded" immediately. They believe in instant gratification; if they can download a song, book, article, or video immediately, why can't everything else come as instantaneously, too?

This generation watched, again and again, as their TVs replayed the horrific sight of planes crashing into the World Trade Center. 9/11 was an important date for anyone from any generation. Yet, because the event took place during the formative years of this generation, it was a pivotal moment in a generation's life. Their generational response? To connect on both a macro and micro scale.

Today, any global event, both positive and negative, is on-line in seconds. Consequently, this generation is as diverse as the globe. When it comes to food choices, politics, sexual orientation, ethnicity, or religion, this generation sees no boundaries.

This was the first generation to be protected by bike helmets, car seats, seat-belt laws, and strong drunk driving laws. The message they took from this was "You are special. We value you." Consequently, this generation values connections. They want to be part of a community—at home, at work, and at play. They will work with their friends at the same company, if they feel this allows them more time with their community; it's about the team. So when someone complains *"Why does Gen Y have to text me 10 times a day?!"* I remind them that Gen Y values connection and, because they are hardwired, texting is their form of communication.

This is a generation of entrepreneurs. They had a voice at "family meetings" from the age of 5, so they have the confidence to articulate their vision, the tech-skills to create their vision, and the community to support them in their vision.

Finally, work and life balance is vital to Gen Y; they saw their parents work endless hours and want none of it. Instead, they want more balance. So an entrepreneurial career path lets them do yoga at 4 p.m. and work at midnight; it's all a continuum to them.

Now that you understand which events shaped this generation and how Gen Y view the world, how can you best connect with them? You use keywords and key phrases that resonate with them. When you do this, they then feel understood and are willing to listen to you. You build rapport, so they will engage with you more willingly. If you continue to use their keywords and key phrases, you will have an effective conversation with them, simply by using their own language.

Keywords and Key Phrases for Gen Y:

- *Global citizen*
- *Balance*
- *Diversity*
- *Community/connections*
- *We/team*

So if you're trying to convince a Gen Y to launch a new Website, you would say something like, *"This will bring together our different stakeholder communities. This feature will allow our members instant access to the information they need. It can be built in stages, so we don't have to work 80-hour weeks for the next 2 months."*

You wouldn't use the same language when trying to convince a Gen X or Boomer to launch a new Website. They have their own keywords and key phrases that resonate best with them. Using the Gen Y keywords and key phrases, and understanding the Gen Y psyche, will help you bridge the cultural gap.

Remember: You will not succeed when trying to change a generational perspective. You will only succeed when tailoring your pitch to each generation. In other words, speak their language. When you do this, they feel more connected to you and more willing to answer your questions. This then helps you overcome their concerns and move forward.

As mentioned before, there are many nuances that impact a person's generational personality. So rather than focusing on the year someone was born, instead focus on her personality. If she shows Boomer traits, even though she is 35 years old, then speak Boomer to her. And if he displays Gen Y tendencies, even though he is 35, then speak Gen Y to him. You'll not only create a rapport and bond with both of these people, you'll also use the language that best resonates with them, helping to create a more effective conversation.

Interact Differently With Each Generation

Language problems, as we just discussed, can create unmanageable situations. In addition, different types of interactions within the generations can also create unmanageable situations. It's easy, when someone from another generation is driving you crazy, to overlook the unique contributions she can make. Instead, pay attention to how each generation prefers to interact. This will help you create a cohesive team.

Baby Boomers

Baby Boomers love face-to-face interactions. They grew up with large groups everywhere, before the age of the Internet. They thrived on mass protests, mass rock concerts, and large families. The idea of IM-ing or texting, when they could be having a face-to-face meeting, is foreign to them. So if you're Generation X or Generation Y, be flexible with Boomers. Try to increase your face-to-face interactions with them—by the water cooler, at meetings, during lunch, and even during coffee breaks. You'll be surprised at how much fun it can be to actually talk live to a person!

Generation X

Gen X grew up between the Baby Boomer face-to-face lifestyle and the Generation Y tech lifestyle. They can be perceived as too independent, too self-focused, and too individualistic. However, another way to look at it is that they are realistic and solution-focused.

Gen Xers often prefer to work alone, on their own timetable, with quick decisions and fast results. So if you're a Baby Boomer or member of Gen Y, be flexible in how you approach Gen X. Don't expect them to work the way you do; be accepting of their different styles. Don't ask them to be involved in every team meeting and every consensus decision; this will only frustrate them. Instead, give them a project that they can work on alone or with only one or two other people. Be decisive in the desired outcomes and clear about your expectations. Then let them get to work. You'll both be amazed at what they can produce when allowed to work in their own style!

Generation Y

Gen Yers were born with a mouse in their hand. They love what technology can do for them and how it connects them to the world, to their friends, and to their family. They love the freedom and creativity it gives them, allowing them to create new ideas in the blink of an eye. That freedom allows them to balance their work and life in ways that no other generation has been able to do before.

So it comes as no surprise that many in Gen Y prefer to interact virtually. To them, an IM chat or a text is the same as a face-to-face meeting. So if you're a Baby Boomer or from Generation X, give them the freedom and flexibility they crave, as long as the job gets done. And it may be time to actually thank them. Even a decade ago, it was unheard of to leave the office early, especially if family matters came up. Now, thanks in part to Gen Y, flex time, remote working, and community service are a normal way of the working life!

◇◇

Appendix A

How Each Generation Can Mentor the Others to Success

Unmanageable situations often create an "us vs. them" mentality, such that one side thinks it knows best and refuses to listen to the other side. Yet it's important to remember that everyone has something to contribute to a team's overall success, and everyone has certain knowledge that can help the organization grow.

The same is true for the generations. Every generation can mentor the others to success, if time is taken to listen.

Baby Boomers

So how can Boomers mentor Gen X and Gen Y? Baby Boomers are extremely skilled at in-person relationships and office politics. They learned how to navigate the huge numbers of personalities in school, on teams, and at work. They understand how the game is played and what to do to succeed at it. They also know one critical skill that Gen Y in particular is missing: when and how to pick up the phone. Yes, the phone. I've seen Gen Yers spend 30 minutes looking for contact information online. In that same time, a Boomer would have called the company, spoken live with the receptionist, found out (because they'd made a personal connection) the best time to reach that person, if the person prefers being contacted by phone or e-mail, if the person uses their full name or a nickname, *and* how to pronounce their name.

Boomers are the masters of this type of networking; Gen X and Gen Y can learn a lot from them in this arena. So let the Boomers mentor on office politics and old-school interpersonal relationships. These are things that are crucial for the ultimate career growth of Gen X and Gen Y.

Gen X

What can Gen X teach Boomers and Gen Y? Gen X often has something that both the Boomers and Gen Y lack: focus.

I know, I know. Boomers and Gen Y think they're focused. But if you look at things unsentimentally (which is what Gen X excels at doing), you'll see that a Boomer's idea of focus is sort of like everyone sitting around a campfire taking their turn discussing the problem. Gen Y's notion of focus is sort of like everyone hanging out at a party taking their turn discussing the problem. And then when everyone has a turn, they both sort of focus on a consensual solution.

The Gen X concept of focus is more like: Problem–Brief Discussion–Decision–Done.

We can all learn from this.

We can also learn from Gen X's perceived cynicism. They see the flaws. They see the problems. They see the things Boomers and Gen Y don't want to see. So put them in charge of being devil's advocate. You'll learn, and your team's work will improve. Let them be your mentors in seeing reality and finding the blind spots. Their perceived cynicism can give others an incredibly important perspective on improving business. Now, that's valuable to any team and organization!

Gen Y

So what can Gen Y teach Boomers and Gen X? Technology! They are the Digital Natives. If you're Gen X, you're a Digital Immigrant. If you're a Boomer, you're the parent of the Digital Immigrant, still living in the old country.

Gen Y was born with technology; they get it. I'm not talking about asking a Gen Y colleague for help with current technology. I'm talking about letting Gen Y show you where technology will be in the next 10 years. They intuitively knew what an "app" was before it was even invented; they also know what technology can do for your organization in the next 20 years. So let them find global best practices and show you the future of technology.

◇◇

Appendix A

Remember: Gen Y wants to be taken seriously. They want their expertise to be acknowledged. Technology is an area where they have expertise, and a vision of what can be accomplished, that the other two generations just can't match because they weren't born with it. So ask for their mentorship in the technology area, and be sure to show your appreciation. You'll not only build innovation and morale, you'll likely save resources in the long run.

Delegating Effectively to Each Generation

Language and ineffective work style interactions can cause unmanageable situations. So can a simple management technique, such as delegation. Most managers tend to delegate in one way; however, each generation actually prefers being delegated to in different ways.

How to Delegate so Boomer Employees Stay Engaged

Boomers are masters of delegation. This generation competed from an early age; there were so many of them, they were always jostling for a place in school, on the team, and in clubs. Consequently, they learned the art of time management and delegation to move up the corporate ladder quickly.

This generation saw the power of using their voice as a group to make a difference, both at a high level and at the detailed level. Not only were they able to successfully advocate for women's rights at a high level, they were also able to finesse the details of policy and legislation to pass laws that would create their vision. This is the beauty of Boomers. They can see both the macro vision and the micro details, and then prioritize to eventually win the battle.

So if you're Gen X or Gen Y, ask Boomers for their expertise on how to prioritize and delegate. They will gladly show you their tips, which will make you more effective and allow you to spend more time with your family.

How to Delegate so Gen X Employees Stay Engaged

If Baby Boomers mastered the art of delegation, Gen X perfected it. That's because Gen X had to be laser focused to navigate their formative years. Between stagflation, high divorce rates, and the humiliation of both the Iran Contra crisis and the *Challenger* explosion, Gen X learned early on to be resourceful and pragmatic when moving forward. Don't forget that this is the era of TQM, Japanese management models, and organizational reengineering. This generation took delegation to the next level, almost automating it.

So if you're a Baby Boomer or a Gen Y, ask your Gen X colleagues for help with laser-focused delegation. Boomers and Gen Yers are so team-focused, they often forget the bottom line, something that Gen X can help them with.

And Gen X: Don't forget that you're sandwiched between two generations that are team-oriented and consensus-driven. So reach out to these groups for input when you're not dealing with a time-sensitive issue; you'll get a wider perspective on the problem at hand.

How to Delegate so Gen Y Employees Stay Engaged

One mistake Baby Boomers and Gen X often make when delegating to Gen Y is that they like to delegate details. Mary might say, *"Hey Juan, can you please update this database?"* without explaining what the database is for. This doesn't go over well with Gen Y because, being Digital Natives, Gen Yers tend to be big-picture thinkers. They have seen globalization, diversity, and technology in ways that no other generation has. They can see the future more clearly than the rest of us, because they understand the current and future use of emerging technology.

So if you're a Baby Boomer or Gen X, before you delegate, ask Gen Y for their ideas by giving them the big picture first. Then allow them to give their input. Remember that they're used to having a voice during "family meetings," so let them have their say at work as well, which will improve their buy-in. They will think nothing of going online and finding out a best practice for a similar project in China, so let Gen Y bring their global thinking to your project. If you let them see the big picture, they will invariably figure out how to make your idea even better. Then start to delegate with them, not to them. I know, it seems like a lot of hand-holding. Yet you'll have a much stronger project once they have understood the big picture and bought into the goal.

So What Does All This Have to Do With Your UE?

Although we have given you **The 5 C Framework**, you know that every UE is different.

Will every UE challenge be caused by generational differences? No. However, in general, if there is a UE challenge, *being unaware of the generational differences will make matters worse for you*.

For example, if your UE is Gen X and you are a Boomer, you might forget that Gen X tends to be pragmatic, cynical, and micro-focused (whereas Boomers tend to be optimistic and team-focused).

This style difference alone could exacerbate the situation. So don't let generational tensions keep your UE from successful change. Be aware of generational differences, and use your knowledge to help your UE.

Understanding generations won't magically solve your UE problem—but it will make things go more smoothly along the way!

Appendix B
The Tools

The "What's it Worth?" Worksheet

Part 1: Cost of the UE's Problem

Estimated Cost of Manager's Time	Hrs./Week	6 Mo. Cost
Time spent with UE		
Time spent with other involved employees		
Time with HR, lawyer or senior management		
Time managing fall-out with clients		
Other		
Total Estimated Cost of Manager's Time		

Estimated Cost of Manager's Time	Hrs./Week	6 Mo. Cost
Estimated Cost of Lost Employee Productivity	Percentage	6 Mo. Cost
Productivity lost by the UE		
Productivity lost by other involved employees		
Other		
Total Estimated Cost of Lost Employee Productivity		

Estimated Direct Costs	Current	6 Mo. Cost
Compensation for product or service mistakes		
Costs of damage to equipment, etc.		
Other		
Total Estimated Direct Costs		

Estimated Opportunity Costs	Current	6 Mo. Cost
Missed deadlines	--	--
Bids not completed	--	--
Projects not developed		
Other	--	--

Estimated Opportunity Costs	Current	6 Mo. Cost
Total Estimated Opportunity Costs, Current and 6-Month		

Part 2: Estimated Cost of "UE Salvage Operation"

Estimated Cost of "UE Salvage Operation"	Hrs./Week	6 Mo. Cost
Manager's Time		
Internal Consultant's Time (HR, legal, etc.)		
External Consultant Evaluation (if desired)		
External Coaching (for UE and/or manager)		
Other		
Total Estimated Cost of "UE Salvage Operation"		
Estimated Cost of UE Replacement (2–2.5 x annual salary)		

Part 3: Benefits of "UE Salvage"

Benefits of "UE Salvage"
Was your UE ever a fully productive employee? If so, what was his/her major contribution?
What would this UE contribute to your team if he/she was functioning fully now?

◇◇

Appendix B

Benefits of "UE Salvage"
What incremental benefits from his/her participation might be captured over time?

The 10 Communications Questions

The 10 Communications Questions
What problem is my UE presenting?
Do I have any sense of the root cause of the problem?
What's the impact on my UE's performance?
What's the impact on my team?
What actions have I taken so far?
How has the UE responded to those actions?
When will I hold a conversation with my UE?
What are the main points I want to get across?
What are the questions I might ask my UE?
How will I know if the talk is a success?

The Trade-Off Tool

The Trade-Off Tool	
Behaviors (sample list)	Fill Out for Each Behavior That Applies
Interactions Attitude Language Deadlines Punctuality Success	My Preference:
	Your Preference:
	The Gap:
	The Solution:

The Perception Gap Tool

The Perception Gap Tool (Use this chart to record intentions, perceptions, and the distance between them.)		
Intention:		
100		100
90		90
80		80
70		70
60		60
50		50
40		40
30		30
20		20
10		10
Perception:		

Goals Diagnostic Chart

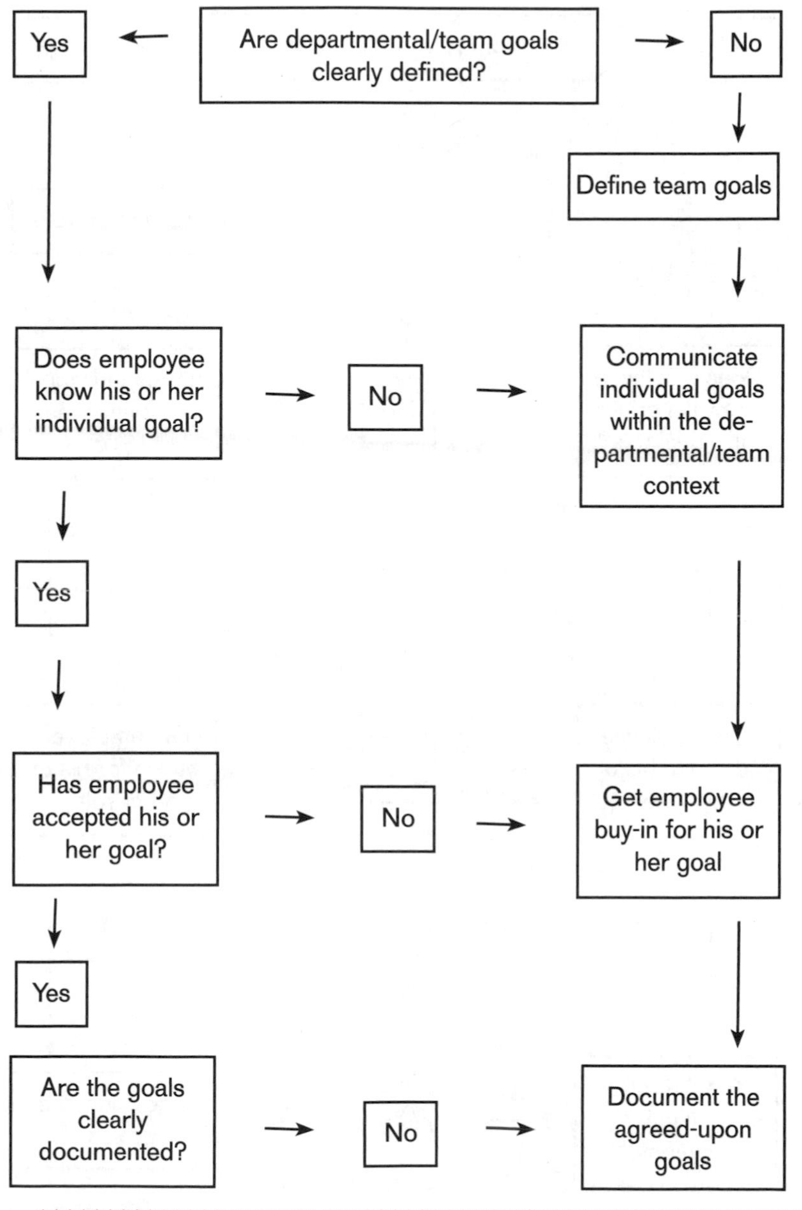

Roles Diagnostic Chart

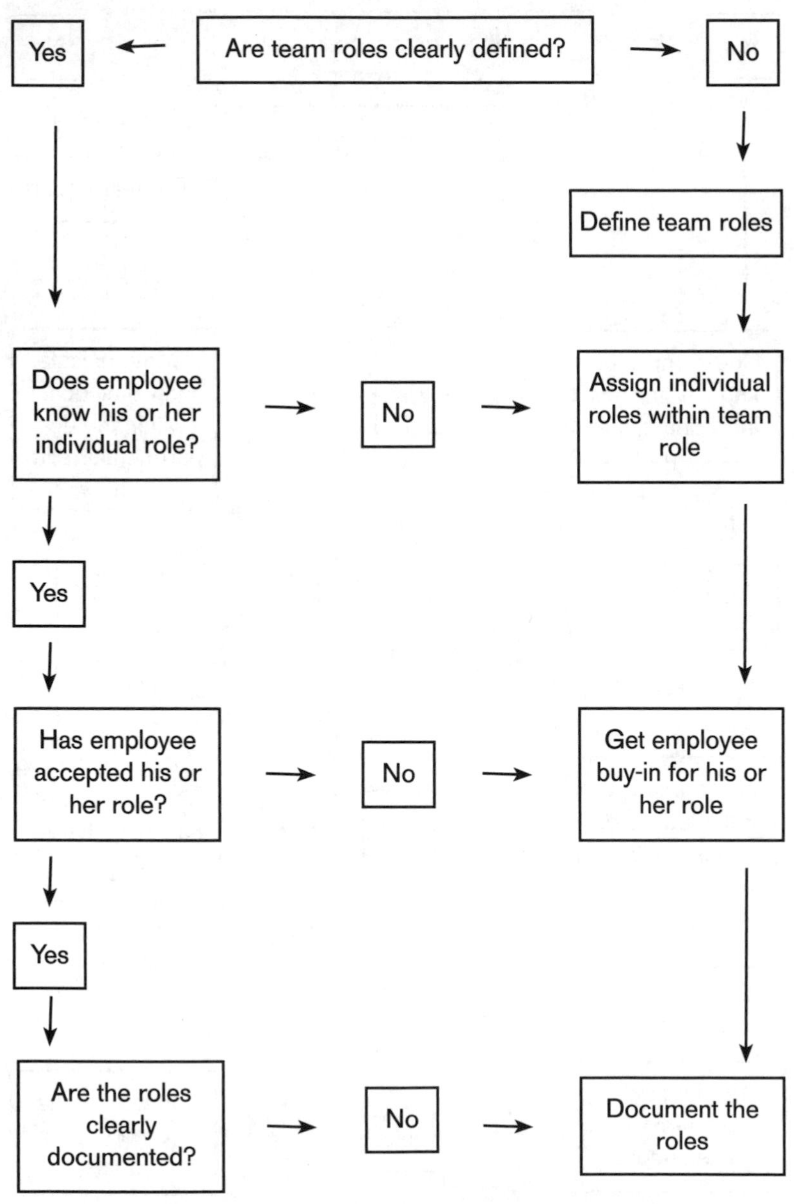

The Balance Tool

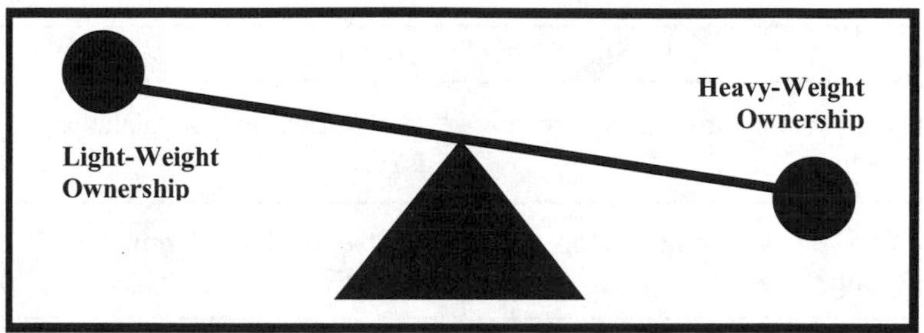

Acknowledgment Checklist

Acknowledgment Checklist	
What did I observe my employee doing right? (Be specific.)	
How is this different, or how does this represent progress, for him or her? (Be specific.)	
Did his or her action produce a positive effect? (Be specific.)	
When will I tell this to him or her?	(Hint: What's wrong with now?)

Coaching Questions

Closed vs. Open-Ended	
"Do you see how this is hurting the team?"	"What impact do you think this has?"
"Are you ever going to stop gossiping?"	"What would be different if this changed?"
"Why are you gossiping about her?!"	"What's the reason for the gossip?"

Advice-Filled vs. Advice-Free	
"Don't you want to stop gossiping?"	"What would happen if you stopped gossiping?"
"Have you decided to change yet?"	"What does changing this look like?"
"Wouldn't you be more successful if you stopped acting like this?!"	"How do you define success?"

Long vs. Short	
"If you had to describe the impact of gossip on your team, and had to explain how you plan to stop it, would you be able to answer that? And what answer would you give?"	"What would the first step to stopping the gossip habit be?'
"In what ways do you think this gossip is contributing to your reputation? And is that reputation congruent with where you see yourself being in this organization two years from now?"	"Where do you want to be in two years?"
"Why do you think that you gossip, and what does your assumption about the underlying cause of your behavior say about your ability to make a change, particularly in the near term?"	"What's the underlying reason?"

The Accountability Tracking Tool

Accountability Tracking Tool (Fill out for each agreed-upon deliverable.)					
Deliverable	**Benchmark Dates**				**Comments**
1. What is being completed?					
2. When will it be completed?					
3. Who will it be delivered to?					
4. Where will it be delivered?					
5. How will it be delivered?					

Bibliography

Elliott, Bob, and Kevin Carroll. *Make Your Point!* Bloomington, Ind.: AuthorHouse, 2005.

Emerson, Brian, and Anne Loehr. *A Manager's Guide to Coaching: Simple and Effective Ways to Get the BEST Out of Your Employees*. New York: AMACOM Books, a division of American Management Association, 2008.

Faber, Adele, and Elaine Mazlish. *How to Talk So Kids Will Listen & Listen So Kids Will Talk*. New York: Harper Paperbacks, 1999.

Fisher, Roger, William L. Ury, and Bruce Patton. *Getting to Yes: Negotiating Agreement Without Giving In*. New York: Penguin (Non-Classics), 2nd Edition, 1991.

Frank, Milo. *How to Get Your Point Across in 30 Seconds or Less*. New York: Pocket Books, a division of Simon & Schuster, 1986.

Kroeger, Otto, with Janet M. Thuesen and Hile Rutledge. *Type Talk at Work: How the 16 Personality Types Determine Your Success on the Job*. New York: Dell Publishing, a division of Random House, 2002.

Mindell, Phyllis, Ed.D. *A Woman's Guide to the Language of Success: Communicating with Confidence and Power*. Paramus, N.J.: Prentice Hall, a Simon & Schuster Company, 1995.

Stone, Douglas, Bruce M. Patton, and Sheila Heen. *Difficult Conversations: How to Discuss What Matters Most*. New York: The Penguin Group, 1999.

Whitworth, Laura, Henry Kimsey-House, and Phil Sandahl. *Co-Active Coaching*. Palo Alto, Calif.: Davies Black Publishing, 1998.

Winget, Larry. *The Idiot Factor: The 10 Ways We Sabotage Our Life, Money and Business*. New York: Gotham Books (The Penguin Group), 2010.

Zeisset, Carolyn. *The Art of Dialogue*. Gainseville, Fla.: Center for the Application of Psychological Type, 2006.

Index

About the Authors

After graduating from Cornell University's School of Hotel Management, **Anne Loehr** owned and managed international, eco-friendly hotels and safari companies for more than 13 years. Frustrated that she couldn't find top-quality leadership programs for her 500 Kenyan employees, Anne honed their management skills herself by creating her own dynamic, team-empowering programs.

Since selling her tourism businesses and becoming a certified coach and management consultant, Anne has been working with executives from diverse organizations, such as Facebook, the U.S. Air Force, Morgan Stanley Smith Barney, the American Red Cross, Johns Hopkins University, Booz Allen Hamilton, John Hancock, the Defense Intelligence Agency, and Merrill Lynch, to help managers improve their communications and deepen their working relationships. The impact? Creative collaboration, improved employee retention, and increased sales.

Named the "Generational Guru" by *The Washington Post*, Anne's work has been featured in *Newsweek International, The Washington Post, National Geographic Traveler, Washingtonian, Body+Soul,* and *CNN Money*. A member of the prestigious National Speakers Association, Anne speaks regularly at national conferences and on the radio. She is also a faculty member at the American Management Association.

Anne co-founded **Safaris for the Soul**, international leadership retreats that help senior managers find their organizational values and purpose. Her first book was *A Manager's Guide to Coaching: Simple and Effective Ways to Get the Best Out of Your Employees*.

Jezra Kaye's lifelong passion for communications began at age 8, when she wrote a spec script for the original *Star Trek*. At 13, she developed a love of classic vocal jazz and began preparing to follow in the footsteps of Ella Fitzgerald, Sarah Vaughn, June Christy, and Carmen McRae. After graduating from high school near Boston, she moved to San Francisco, where she studied social psychology at UC Berkeley and sang with Top 40, jazz, and Latin bands. Returning to Boston six years later, Jezra enrolled in the renowned New England Conservatory of Music, where she earned a Bachelor of Music degree (the world's best training for a speechwriter) and met her husband, Jerome Harris.

After moving to Brooklyn in 1981, Jezra entered the marketing communications field. As a corporate speechwriter and creative director, she worked with Fortune 500 executives to design, develop, and stage internal conferences whose goals ranged from educating employees to motivating salespeople to creating consensus among top global leaders. In this role, Jezra prepared executives for their stage presentations and wrote materials that ranged from keynote speeches to high-concept videos to "book shows" (small theatrical productions) that dramatized a company's products or services. Her work with brand managers, medical directors, business consultants, and CEOs prepared Jezra to serve her own diverse and high-powered clientele.

Today, as president of **Speak Up for Success**, Jezra shares the power of confident, authentic communications with women and men who have important things to say. Her keynote speeches, workshops, and individual speaker coaching have helped countless businesspeople and professionals perform more effectively, negotiate more powerfully, and advocate with confidence for their clients' needs and their own career growth.